THE
LIFE

DEDICATION

To
Myra, Cathy, and Kathy

THE FAITH SERIES

THE FAITH
Understanding Orthodox Christianity

THE WAY
*What Every Protestant Should Know
about the Orthodox Church*

THE TRUTH
*What Every Roman Catholic Should Know
about the Orthodox Church*

THE LIFE
The Orthodox Doctrine of Salvation

THE
LIFE

The Orthodox Doctrine of Salvation

Clark Carlton

ISBN-10 1-928653-02-2

ISBN-13 978-1-928653-02-8

Cover Photo: Cristo tra Arcangeli Galta placida
Revenna Italy. Used by permission

All Scripture Quotations are from the King James
Version unless otherwise noted. Some quotations
have been emended by the author to better reflect
the original Greek text.

Regina Orthodox Press
P.O. Box 5288
Salisbury, MA 01952
1-800-636-2470
FAX: 978-462-5079

www.reginaorthodoxpress.com

CONTENTS

CONTENTS

Part Two
Topical Studies

ABOUT THE AUTHOR

Clark Carlton was born in Cookeville, Tennessee in 1964 and reared as a Southern Baptist. He earned a B.A. in philosophy from Carson-Newman College in Jefferson City, Tennessee. While studying as a Raymond Bryan Brown Memorial Scholar at the Southeastern Baptist Theological Seminary in Wake Forest, North Carolina, he converted to the Orthodox Faith and was chrismated at the St. Gregory the Great Orthodox Mission in Raleigh. The story of his conversion is recounted in *The Way: What Every Protestant Should Know about the Orthodox Church.*

Mr. Carlton earned a Master of Divinity degree from St. Vladimir's Orthodox Theological Seminary in Crestwood, New York in 1990. His senior thesis, under the direction of Fr. John Meyendorff, was entitled "The Humanity of Christ According to St. Maximus the Confessor."

In 1993, he earned an M.A. in Early Christian Studies from the Catholic University of America in Washington, D.C. At present he is working as an adjunct instructor of philosophy at Tennessee Technological University in his home town while completing his Ph.D. dissertation on the dogmatic and ascetical theology of St. Mark the Monk (5th c.). With this volume, Mr. Carlton completes his four-volume *Faith Series.*

ACKNOWLEDGMENTS

"No one is saved alone." So goes a popular saying among Orthodox theologians. We are not saved merely as individuals, but as members of Christ's Body, the Church. As such, I owe an unpayable debt of gratitude to many people in the Church, who have been beacons of light and examples of Christ.

First of all I must thank several *non-orthodox* Christians, notably the pastors and Sunday school teachers of the First Baptist Church of Cookeville, Tennessee and the members of the youth department of the Tennessee Baptist Convention. Had it not been for their love, I might not be Orthodox today.

Secondly, I need to thank the faithful priests that have helped me along the way. Fr. Vladimir Demshuk, who received me into Holy Orthodoxy, my seminary classmate and now my "official" pastor, Fr. Andrew Davis, my "unofficial" pastors, Frs. Gordon Walker and Stephen Rogers, and my spiritual father, Archimandrite Damian.

Lastly I would like to thank two dear brothers in Christ who have been of invaluable help in preparing this book, James J. Condra, Esq. of Birmingham, Alabama and Mr. Theron Mathis of Louisville, Kentucky. Like myself, Theron is a former Baptist seminarian who has found the Pearl of Great Price.

Clark (Innocent) Carlton
Feast of the Protection of the Theotokos, 2000

INTRODUCTION

What is Salvation?

For the grace of God that bringeth salvation hath appeared to all men, teaching us that, denying ungodliness and worldly lusts, we should live soberly, righteously, and godly, in this present world; Looking for that blessed hope, and the glorious appearing of the great God and our Saviour Jesus Christ; Who gave Himself for us, that He might redeem us from all iniquity, and purify unto Himself a peculiar people, zealous of good works (Titus 2:11-14).

There is no more important or pressing issue for each person to consider than that of his own salvation. But, what do we mean by salvation? We hear so many different versions — from televangelists to bumper stickers — we may well wonder if any two people mean exactly the same thing by the term. For some, salvation means little more than avoiding a fiery place of terror called hell when one dies. For others, it means access to a celestial Disneyland, where one will enjoy great riches. For others, salvation has been "demythologized" and "psychoanalyzed" down to a *feeling* of emotional stability and peace in this life, irregardless of what may or may not happen in the next (*if* there is a next life).

While religious fads come and go and people seek their salvation in this or that new leader or idea, the Orthodox Christian Church has proclaimed the same message for almost two thousand years. Each and every human person was created to live in an intimate union with God, sharing in His eternal, divine life, becoming through participation what He is by nature.

This union with God, however, is possible only because God has taken the initiative: *God bowed the heavens and came down* (Psa. 17[18]:9). There was no way for man to raise himself up to God, so God came to man in the person of His Only-begotten Son, the eternal Word of God. "God became man, that man might become divine." This theme is repeated again and again throughout the history of the Church. It is the *raison d'être* of Orthodox Christianity.

Because Orthodoxy defines salvation as union with God, there are many differences between the way the Orthodox approach the subject and the way Roman Catholics and Protestants approach it. Many of the controversies that have vexed Roman Catholics and Protestants since the sixteenth century are simply non-issues for the Orthodox.

Nevertheless, for most Americans and Western Europeans — including even Orthodox Christians — the Orthodox doctrine of salvation seems strange. This is because our conceptual framework has been shaped by the Reformation and the subsequent history of Western Christianity. In other words, we are *accustomed* to thinking in the categories bequeathed to us by medieval theologians such as Anselm of Canterbury and by

Reformers such as Luther and Calvin. This framework has been further reinforced by the popularity of Evangelicalism. Who among us has not heard Billy Graham preach at least once?

Orthodoxy sounds strange to our ears because it presupposes a different conceptual framework than the one we are used to. The Orthodox simply do not approach the question of salvation from the same perspective as Roman Catholics and Protestants. This fact presents several problems for anyone undertaking an explanation of the Orthodox doctrine of salvation. There is no way to present the Orthodox doctrine without some reference to the non-orthodox ideas that prevail in our culture. Yet, by constantly referring to prevailing ideas, one runs the risk of distorting the Orthodox doctrine in an effort to make it "understandable" to Western readers.

I have divided this volume into two parts. In part one, *The Homeland of Your Heart's Desire*, I present the Orthodox doctrine of salvation on its own terms, with as few references as possible to non-orthodox ideas.[1] In part two, I present a series of topical studies on various issues relating to salvation. In these studies I address directly various non-orthodox ideas and explain why they are unacceptable from an Orthodox perspective.

I strongly urge the non-orthodox reader to read the first part first, even though he or she may be tempted to skip to the chapter on Faith vs. Works. Even if the

[1] An abridged version of this is available as a separate volume designed specifically for evangelistic purposes. *Homeland of Your Heart's Desire* (Salisbury, MA: Regina Orthodox Press, 2000).

reader gets no more than a "general impression" of Orthodoxy from the first part, that will be an invaluable help in understanding the chapters in part two.

With this volume I conclude the *Faith Series*. In many ways, this volume and the first, *The Faith*, form bookends. *The Life* is intended to be more *explanatory* and less polemical than the middle volumes, *The Way* and *The Truth*. For this reason I have not undertaken an exhaustive refutation of non-orthodox ideas about salvation. Rather, my hope is that the reader will be able to understand Orthodoxy as a thing in and of itself, not simply in relation to Roman Catholicism or Protestantism, both of which are predated by Orthodoxy.

PART ONE

THE
HOMELAND
OF YOUR
HEART'S DESIRE

CHAPTER ONE

The Creation of Man

It was not Paradise
that gave rise to the creation of mankind;
rather, it was for Adam alone
that Paradise had been planted,
for to its buds Adam's heart is superior,
to its fruits and words,
because rational speech has more savor
than the produce of Paradise;
truth in mankind
surpasses its plants,
and love is likewise more comely
than its sweet scents.[1]

The book of Genesis in the Old Testament recounts the story of the creation of the world and of man in particular. Our quest to understand the reason for our existence—and the very notion of salvation—begins, therefore, with the first book of the Bible.

The first verse states, *In the beginning God created the heavens and the earth* (Genesis 1:1). The writer of Genesis goes on to tell us that God created the sun and moon and stars and all of the wonderful things that fill up the

---

[1] St. Ephrem the Syrian, *Hymns on Paradise* VI:6, tr. by Sebastian Brock (Crestwood, NY: SVS Press, 1990), pp. 110-111.

earth. In short, God created everything that exists, including man. But Genesis tells us something else about man, something that is not said of any other creature; man was created in the image of God:

> Then God said, "Let us make man in Our image, after Our likeness" . . . So God created man in His own image; in the image of God He created him; male and female He created them (Genesis 1:26-27).

The Orthodox doctrine of salvation is rooted in the doctrine of creation. Notice, however, that two different words are used in this passage, *image* (εἰκὼν) and *likeness* (ὁμοίωσις).[2] Many Fathers understood this to mean that there is a distinction between man as he was originally created and the final goal of man's life. Man is created in the image of God, but He is called to grow into the likeness of God by the use of his free will. St. Diadochos of Photiki wrote,

> All men are made in God's image; but to be in His likeness is granted only to those who through great love have brought their own freedom into subjection to God. For only when we do not belong to ourselves do we become like Him who through love has reconciled us to Himself. No one achieves this unless he per-

---

[2] For a scholarly discussion see Vladimir Lossky, "The Theology of the Image" in *In the Image and Likeness of God* (Crestwood, NY: SVS Press, 1985), pp. 125-139.

suades his soul not to be distracted by the false glitter of this life.[3]

Thus, there is an inherent dynamism in the creation of man. Man was created with a goal: to be conformed to the likeness of God. This is confirmed by St. Paul in the New Testament, when he writes:

For whom He did foreknow, He also did predestinate to be conformed to the image of His Son, that He might be the firstborn among many brethren (Rom 8:29).

And again,

My little children, of whom I travail in birth again until Christ be formed in you (Gal. 4:19).

Man's salvation, then, is founded upon his creation in the image of God. But, what does it mean to be created in the image of God? Throughout the centuries people have given different answers to this question. Some have thought that it is in man's ability to reason or to communicate that the image of God is to be found. Others have suggested that God's image is revealed in man's ability to create or to govern. All of these answers are correct to a certain extent, for the image of

---

[3] "On Spiritual Knowledge and Discrimination: One Hundred Texts," 4 in Palmer, Sherrard, and Ware, *The Philokalia*, vol. 1 (London: Faber and Faber, 1979), 253. See also St. Maximus the Confessor: "Every rational nature indeed is made to the image of God; but only those who are good and wise are made to His likeness." "Centuries on Charity," 3:25 in *Maximus Confessor:Selected Writings*, tr. by George Berthold (NY: Paulist Press, 1985), p. 64.

God in us is the totality of our human existence, that is, everything that makes us *persons*.

The term, *person,* is difficult to define because people by nature defy definition. We can classify people according to age or height or race or sex, but these things cannot begin to explain the mystery of *personhood*. If you have ever loved another person, then you know that it is impossible to completely understand and classify a human being, no matter how hard we may try. Although we cannot fully define what a person is, we can say at least three things about personhood that will help us understand what it means for us to be created in the image of God: a person is free, unique, and relational.

According to the Bible, there was no necessity for God to create anything. He created the world out of *freedom*. As persons created in the image of God, we too are free. God did not create us as robots; rather, He endowed us with freedom. God created us with the potential to grow, to become ever more like Him through the use of our free will. This freedom to grow, however, also entails the freedom to reject God. God will not force Himself on anyone. Whether we fulfill our human vocation and live according to the image of God or whether we reject God is up to each of us:

> I call heaven and earth to record this day against you, that I have set before you life and death, blessing and cursing; therefore choose life that both thou and thy descendants may live (Deuteronomy 30:19).

As persons created in the image of God we are not only free, we are also unique and unrepeatable. Just as no two fingerprints are exactly alike, so no two people are exactly alike. Of course, our society often tries to suppress our uniqueness. Indeed, it seems as though our human identity is reduced to our Social Security number. Yet no matter how dehumanizing modern life may be, it can never suppress the absolute uniqueness of the human person, for that uniqueness is the imprint of God upon us all. God calls us all to grow into His likeness, but in a way that is unique to each of us. It is sin that forces upon us a sterile uniformity, reducing us to a life of mere animal existence. But God would have us to share in His eternity, to grow ever more like Him in a way uniquely our own. The French aviator and author, Antoine de Saint-Exupéry, describes our personal uniqueness in a beautiful way in his book, *The Little Prince*. In the book, a small fox teaches the Little Prince about the mystery of personhood:

> To me [said the fox], you are still nothing more than a little boy who is just like a hundred thousand other little boys. And I have no need of you. And you, on your part, have no need of me. To you, I am nothing more than a fox like a hundred thousand other foxes. But if you tame me, then we shall need each other. To me, you will be unique in all the world. To you, I shall be unique in all the world.[4]

---

[4](NY: Harvest/HJV Edition, 1971), p. 80.

This quotation from *The Little Prince* illustrates the third important aspect of personhood: our personal uniqueness is found only in a relationship of love with other persons. There is a great deal of difference between an individual and a person. An individual is a number, a member of a set, "a little boy like a hundred thousand other little boys." A person, on the other hand, loves and is loved. It is the ability to love that ultimately defines us as persons created in the image of God. A man who stands alone and self-sufficient is not a person--is not fully human. As the English churchman and poet John Donne wrote, "No man is an island entire of himself." You cannot be a person--that is to say, fully human--on your own. To be human is to relate to others. There are three important relationships that define us as persons: our relationship with God, our relationship with other people, and our relationship with the physical world.

According to the book of Genesis, God created us for a relationship of love and communion with Himself. There is a sense in which our relationship to God is more primary than even our relationship to our biological parents, for *the Lord God formed man of the dust of the ground, and breathed into his nostrils the breath of life; and man became a living soul* (Genesis 2:7). What is more, God is not only the originator of human life, He is the source of eternal life. As creatures, we are made from the dust of the ground; we have no life in ourselves. As a great, Russian bishop of the 19th century[5] said, "All

---

[5] Metropolitan Philaret of Moscow.

creatures are balanced upon the creative Word of God, as if upon a bridge of diamond; above them is the abyss of divine infinitude, below them that of their own nothingness." Only in communion with God, the Creator and source of life, do we have the promise of everlasting life. *And this is life eternal, that they might know Thee, the only true God, and Jesus Christ Whom Thou hast sent* (John17:3).

As creatures of God, then, our most basic relationship is with the One Who created us. But the book of Genesis goes on to tell us that God looked upon the man He had created and said, *It is not good that man should be alone* (Genesis 2:18). Thus, Eve was created that Adam's life might be complete. As persons created in the image of God, we were created not only for communion with God, but with one another as well. In fact, we cannot be fully human apart from our relationships with others.

Human relationships are important because our lives are deeply bound up with the lives of other people. All human beings, regardless of sex, race, or background, share the same basic human nature. You might say that "under the skin" we are all just alike. Yet each one of us expresses our humanity in a way which is uniquely our own. To love another person is to discover what is unique about that person and to express our own uniqueness, while at the same time affirming our common humanity. This helps us to understand the commandment to love our neighbors as ourselves. This does not mean that we should love other people *to the extent that* we love ourselves; rather it is in loving others that we discover our own selves. On the other hand, to hate another person is an act of suicide; it is a denial of our common humanity.

In addition to our relationships with God and with one another, the Genesis narrative tells us about a third relationship which defines us as persons created in the image of God: our relationship with the physical world. *Then God said, "Let Us make man in Our image, after Our likeness; let them have dominion over the fish of the sea, and over the fowl of the air, and over the cattle, and over all the earth, and over every creeping thing that creepeth upon the earth* (Genesis 1:26). We were created to "rule" the earth, not in a tyrannical way, but rather as images of God. In other words, we are to govern the earth in love, to take care of the physical world that God has given to us.

We are to enter into a personal relationship with the world and bring it into our relationship with God:

> *Out of the ground the Lord God formed every beast of the field and every fowl of the air, and brought them unto Adam to see what he would call them. And whatsoever Adam called every living creature, that was the name thereof* (Genesis 2:19).

In the Bible, a name is much more than a tag to distinguish one thing from another. A name reveals something about the very essence of a thing. Thus, to name something implies a deep, personal knowledge of that thing. This may be difficult to understand, so let us take a common example from daily life: the family pet. Now the family pet is not like an ordinary dog or cat. We give it a personal name. Although it is not a person, we somehow *personalize* it through our love for it. In this way, it is no longer simply something we own; it is a part of the family. Similarly, we are to personalize all of creation, including the rocks and rivers, and to bring it into our "family" — our relationship of love with God and with one another.

These relationships, then, are what define us as persons created in the image of God. As we said at the beginning, however, the Orthodox conception of the image of God is dynamic not static. Indeed, the very notion of "relationship" implies growth. We are created in God's image, but we are called to *grow* into the likeness of God. The more we live out our humanity in the way in which God intended, the more like God we become. Fr. Dimitru Staniloae, a Romanian priest, sums up our vocation as human beings quite well: "The glory to which man is called is that he should grow more god-like by growing ever more human."

CHAPTER ONE

Reflection

1. What, according to the Book of Genesis, is the difference between man and all other creatures?

2. What is the difference between the *image* and *likeness* of God?

3. What is it about the human person that is in the likeness of God?

4. Is a person the same as an individual?

5. Did God have to create the world? What does this say about human nature?

6. What three relationships define the being of each human?

7. What is the most important relationship in a person's life?

8. What does our common human nature say about how we should relate to each other?

9. What does Adam's "naming of the animals" say about man's vocation?

10. Should human nature be described as static or dynamic?

The Fall of Man

*But men, having turned from the contemplation
of God to evil of their own devising, had come
inevitably under the law of death. Instead of
remaining in the state in which God had created them, they were in process of becoming
corrupted entirely, and death had them completely under its dominion. For the transgression of the commandment was making them
turn back again according to their nature; and
as they had at the beginning come into being
out of non-existence, so were they now on the
way to returning, through corruption to non-
existence again. The presence and love of the
Word had called them into being; inevitably,
therefore, when they lost the knowledge of God,
they lost existence with it; for it is God alone
Who exists, evil is non-being, the negation and
antithesis of good.[1]*

The description of man's life in the first two chapters of Genesis is called "Paradise." But you and I do
not live in Paradise, and neither did the person who

---

[1] St. Athanasius of Alexandria, *On the Incarnation* I:4 (Crestwood, NY: SVS Press, 1982), pp. 29-30.

wrote the book of Genesis. That is why the very next chapter of Genesis describes the Fall of man. This story tells us why we do not experience life as God intended for it to be.

On the surface, the story seems rather simple and straightforward. God told Adam and Eve that they could eat of every tree of the Garden except one. When they disobeyed God, they were expelled from Paradise. Yet this seemingly simple act of disobedience reflects something far more profound than the mere breaking of a rule. According to the story, the serpent tempted Eve by telling her that if she ate the fruit of the Tree of Knowledge, she would be like God (Genesis 3:4). Now we know that man was created in the image of God in order to share in God's life; so there was nothing wrong or sinful in Eve's desire to be like God. Indeed, this is the desire within all of us for fulfillment and happiness. The problem lies in the fact that Adam and Eve tried to become like God *without* God. They turned to the fruit of creation for knowledge and life and fulfillment rather than to the One Who had created all things and is the only source of life. The Apostle Paul summed up the matter when he said that man has *exchanged the truth of God for the lie, and worshiped and served the creature rather than the Creator* (Romans 1:25).

God created man in His own image that man might enjoy communion with Him and thereby have unending life. To this end, the world was given to man not only as a source of biological life, but as a means of communion with God. In eating the "forbidden fruit," however, man rejected both his own vocation and that

26

of creation by making what is created the object of his desire. Fr. Alexander Schmemann wrote that the forbidden tree "is the image of the world loved for itself, and the eating of it is the image of life understood as an end in itself."[2]

In the same way, we also look to this world to give us life and fulfillment. We try to find meaning in our lives somewhere within creation rather than in our Creator. All of this places us in a rather ironic situation: by making the life of this world an end in itself, we ignore the Creator of this world, Who is the only source of true and everlasting life. Thus, the first and most devastating effect of sin is that it separates us from communion with God. Or rather, *we* separate *ourselves* from Him.

The rebellion of Adam and Eve is man's collective "No Thank you" to God and, therefore, man's collective act of suicide. By estranging ourselves from the only source of true life we confine ourselves to this present life which is, in the words of Shakespeare's Macbeth, "a walking shadow, a poor player who struts and frets his hour upon the stage and then is heard no more." In short, we have become enslaved to death. From a biological point of view, of course, death is quite natural. But we are more than mere biological organisms; we were created in God's image as persons who are able to relate and to love. And for persons, death is always a tragedy for it means the loss of someone unique and unrepeatable, someone who loves and is loved. Death

[2]*For the Life of the World* (Crestwood: SVS Press, 1973), p. 17.

makes of human life a "tale told by an idiot, full of sound and fury, signifying nothing." All of our attempts to find meaning in this world are swallowed up by the grave. Death is a terrifying tragedy because it brings the end of *this* life, and this is the *only* life we know. The curse pronounced upon Adam and Eve is pronounced upon each one of us: *For dust thou art, and unto dust shalt thou return* (Genesis 3:19).

Once man made the world into an object of his desires it did not take long for him to turn against his fellow men and use them as tools to accomplish his purposes. Thus, the second effect of sin is that it destroys our human relationships. It is no accident that the story of the Fall of man in chapter three of Genesis is immediately followed by the story of Cain and Abel—the first murder—in chapter four. As a race, we are beset by envy, jealousy, hate, lust, greed, and all of the other things that prevent us from building and maintaining loving relationships with others. We witness this at every level of human life. We pride ourselves on our technological achievements, yet in this advanced and "enlightened" century more than 50 million people have been systematically executed by their *own* governments.

On the level of interpersonal relationships, the divorce rate and crime statistics speak for themselves. Our "civilized" society is filled with abused children and battered wives, with runaway teenagers and homeless adults. To be sure, our society has made great advances over the centuries. Medical science has enabled us to live longer—but for what? Can the quality of our lives be measured by the quality of our television reception?

The third major consequence of sin is that it alters our perception of the world in which we live. Instead of viewing the world as a gift of God, given for communion with Him, we have made of the world an object for the fulfillment of our desires. Just as we use one another as a means to achieve our desires, so we have turned the world into a tool used for our own ends. We are only now beginning to realize the damage that our greed has done to the environment. In our self-centeredness we have treated the world as if it were a disposable commodity. The problem is that this is the only world we have.

Consider, therefore, the horrible irony of our situation. We were created in the image of God to live in a perfect communion of love with God, with one another, and with the entire created order. Yet in our self-centeredness we have abandoned the only true source of life and love. We have sealed ourselves off from one another within the impregnable fortresses of our own egos. And we have turned a garden of delight into a toxic waste dump. We were born to be kings and queens, but instead we live as paupers in a slum of our own making, fighting each other for a few scraps of bread that will keep us alive for only a short while.

Jesus told a story about a young man, the son of a wealthy nobleman, who decided that life in his father's house was not for him. So, taking his share of the estate, he set out on his own. Things went pretty well for a while; he had a good time until the money ran out. But then, he ended up working for a farmer, slopping pigs. While in the pigsty he "came to himself" — he remembered his noble birth and realized the depths to which he had sunk. At that moment he resolved to return to his father's house and beg to be taken back as a servant. If you think about it, a "pigsty" is a good description of the mess we have made of the world. The story of the prodigal son is the story of each one of us. As the Apostle Paul said, *all have sinned and come short of the glory of God* (Romans 3:23).

The Good News that the Church proclaims is that man *can* go home again! The father received the prodigal son with open arms and restored him to his place of honor. So also will God the Father receive all who come to him in faith and love. Jesus Christ can raises mankind up out of the pigsty and lead us back to the house of the Father. *I am the way, the truth, and the life. No man cometh unto the Father but by me* (John 14;6). Let us now consider the person and work of Jesus Christ and learn how He is able to restore us to communion with God the Father.

Reflection

1. Do we experience life as God intended for it to be? Why or why not?

2. Was it wrong for Adam and Eve to want to be like God?

3. What was the real sin of Adam and Eve?

4. The eating of the forbidden fruit is a symbol of what?

5. Did God "kill" Adam and Eve for their sin?

6. What is the meaning of death?

7. What is the second major consequence of sin?

8. In what ways do we experience this in our own lives?

9. What is the third major consequence of sin?

10. What lesson does the story of the Prodigal Son teach us?

The Person and Work of Christ

Blessed be the Child Who today delights Bethlehem.

Blessed be the Newborn Who today made humanity young again.

Blessed be the Fruit Who bowed Himself down for our hunger.

Blessed Be the Gracious One Who suddenly enriched all of our poverty and filled our need.

Blessed be He Whose mercy inclined Him to heal our sickness.[1]

Jesus once asked His disciples, *Whom do men say that I, the Son of Man, am* (Matthew 16:13-19)? They replied that some people thought He was a prophet and that others thought He was John the Baptist returned from the dead. Then Jesus asked them, *But whom say ye that I am?* This is a question that each one of us must answer

---

[1] St. Ephrem the Syrian, "Hymns on the Nativity," 3 in *Ephrem the Syrian: Hymns*, tr. by Kathleen McVey (NY: Paulist Press, 1989), pp. 82-83.

for himself, for what we think of Jesus Christ and how we relate to Him will determine how we relate to God. Today, almost all people recognize Jesus as a great, spiritual teacher. Moslems consider Him a prophet; Jews, Buddhists, and even atheists admire His ethical teaching. Yet Jesus, Himself, never wrote anything; nor did He come to give us a new philosophy or found a school. The primary importance of Jesus Christ lies in *Who* He is and what He *did*.

The Apostle Peter, who at that time was called Simon, answered, *Thou art the Christ, the Son of the Living God.* Jesus replied, *Blessed art thou, Simon Bar-Jonah, for flesh and blood hath not revealed it unto you, but My Father Who is in heaven.* Simon Peter's confession tells us two things about Jesus Christ: He is the Christ — that is, the Messiah of the Jewish People — and the Son of God. In fact, He is the Messiah *because* He is the Son of God. Let us consider this more closely.

The Messiah of the Jewish People

The book of Genesis tells us that God was not willing for His good creation to simply dissolve back into nothingness after the Fall. "For Thou dost not wish, O Master, that the work of Thy hands should perish; neither dost Thou take pleasure in the destruction of men, but Thou desirest that all should be saved and come to the knowledge of the Truth."[2] For this reason, God established a covenant, or agreement, with an ancient people, Israel. To the People of Israel — the Jews — God

[2] A prayer of St. Basil the Great.

gave the Ten Commandments and sent prophets to proclaim His will. The Old Testament tells of the mighty wonders that God did in the midst of this people in order to display His power and demonstrate His love for them.

Through the Law, the prophets, and all of His mighty deeds for Israel, God was preparing the way for the One Who would be able to bring the Truth of God and the gift of eternal life not just to Israel, but to the entire world. This long-expected Savior was called the "Messiah." When the Apostle Peter confessed Jesus to be the "Christ," he was confessing Him to be the long-awaited hope of Israel and of all the peoples of the world.[3]

Of course, not everyone realized this at the time. Many people were expecting the Messiah to be a political or military leader who would deliver Israel from the oppression of the Roman Empire. But these people did not realize that what holds all of humanity captive is not a political power, but our own self-centeredness and enslavement to death. Jesus Christ, the Messiah sent by God, is far more powerful than any political or military leader. He is the Son of God Himself. God did not send a messenger or intermediary to deliver mankind; He came in person—the person of His Only-begotten Son. In the past God spoke to men at various times and in many different ways through His prophets, but with the coming of Christ, He *hath in these last days spoken unto us by His Son, Whom He hath appointed*

[3]"Christ" is the Greek translation of "Messiah."

Heir of all things, by Whom also He made the worlds (Hebrews 1:1-2).

The Son of God

Jesus Christ is the Son of God. He is also referred to in the New Testament as the Word of God. There was never a time when He did not exist. In fact, the concept of time is really inapplicable, since time is an aspect of creation. God exists outside of time; He is the Creator of time. From all eternity God exists with His Son (or Word) and His Spirit. Thus, the one Godhead is not some impersonal intellect or absolute idea, but rather a Trinity of divine Persons: God the Father dwelling eternally with His Son and His Spirit. God the Father sent His Son into the world in order to bring the world back into communion with Himself. *God was in Christ reconciling the world unto Himself* (2 Corinthians 5:18).

The Gospel of Luke recounts for us the story of Jesus' human conception and birth. The Holy Spirit came upon a young virgin named Mary and she conceived. From her, the Son and Word of God took upon Himself our human nature. He became like us in every way, while remaining God. Thus, Jesus Christ is both God and man, uniting in Himself both humanity and divinity so that we too might share in the divine life of God. There are four important things that we can say about the fact that God has become man.

First, because Jesus Christ is the Son of God made man, He is able to reveal God to us in a way that no prophet or holy man ever could. St. Athanasius asked,

For of what use is existence to the creature if it cannot know its Maker? How could men be reasonable beings if they had no knowledge of the Word and Reason of the Father, through Whom they had received their being? They would be no better than the beasts, had they no knowledge save of earthly things; and why should God have made them at all, if He had not intended them to know Him?

Before His death and resurrection, Jesus told His disciples that He was going to His Father. Philip asked Him, *Lord, show us the Father* (John 14:8-10). Jesus replied, *Have I been so long time with you, and yet hast thou not known me, Philip? He that hath seen Me hath seen the Father . . . Believest thou not that I am in the Father, and the Father in Me? The words that I speak unto you I speak not of myself; but the Father Who dwelleth in Me, He doeth the works.* No one has ever seen God the Father, yet Jesus Christ brings us face to face with Him. St. Maximus wrote:

> In becoming incarnate, the Word of God teaches us the mystical knowledge of God because He shows us in Himself the Father and the Holy Spirit. For the full Father and the full Holy Spirit are essentially and completely in the full Son, even the incarnate Son, without being themselves incarnate.[4]

---

[4] *Commentary on the Our Father* 2 in *Maximus Confessor: Selected Writings*, p. 103.

Second, because Christ is the eternal Image of the Father's Person (cf. Col. 1:15 and Heb. 1:3), He alone is able to renew the image of God in man. St. Irenaeus speaks of Christ "recapitulating" in humanity in Himself, in a sense recreating humanity. St. Athanasius wrote,

> What, then was god to do? What else could He possibly do, being God, but renew His Image in mankind, so that through it men might once more come to know Him? ... You know what happens when a portrait that has been painted on a panel becomes obliterated through external stains. The artist does not throw away the panel, but the subject of the portrait has to come and sit for it again, and then the likeness is re-drawn on the same material. Even so was it with the All-holy Son of God. He, the Image of the Father, came and dwelt in our midst, in order that He might renew mankind made after Himself, and seek out His lost sheep...[5]

Remember that we said in chapter one that the image of God in man is dynamic. Man was created to grown in the likeness of God. In recreating the image of God in man, Christ once again opens the possibility for our growth into the likeness of God. Indeed, we not only have the possibility of becoming *like* God, but of being united with Him. This brings us to the third thing that we can say about the incarnation.

---

[5] *On the Incarnation* 13-14, pp. 41-42.

CHAPTER THREE

Because the Son of God has assumed our human nature He has united it with His divine nature. This means that we, who are creatures, are able to share in the life and glory of God Himself. In the words of the Apostle Peter, we are able to become *partakers of the divine nature* (2 Peter 1:4). This does not mean that we will one day be absorbed into God and lose our personal identity. On the contrary, it means that we as unique persons created in the image of God will be able to share in God's eternity and enjoy life beyond the limitations of our creaturely existence. Here is a beautiful passage from St. Maximus:

> If the Word of God and God the Son of the Father became son of man and man Himself for this reason, to make men gods and sons of God, then we must believe that we shall be where Christ is now as head of the whole body having become in His human nature a forerunner to the Father on our behalf. For God will be in the "assembly of the gods (Psalm 81[82]2:1)," that is, of those who are saved, standing in their midst and apportioning there the ranks of blessedness without any spatial distance separating Him from the elect.[6]

Fourth, because Jesus Christ led a sinless life in full communion with God, He has opened the way for us to live life as it was meant to be. Jesus Christ led a human life in every way like ours except for one thing: He

[6] *Chapters on Knowledge* 2:25 in *Maximus Confessor: Selected Writings*, pp. 152-153.

never gave in to the temptation of pride and self-centeredness that so dominates our lives. Because of this, He remained in full communion with His Father and lived a natural, human life in the manner in which God originally intended. In fact, one could say that Jesus was the first truly human *person* because He was the first to realize human life in perfect communion with God. In doing so, He has made it possible for us to return to the Father's house and live the life He intends for us. *I am come that they might have life, and that they might have it more abundantly* (John 10:10).

The meaning of the person and work of Jesus Christ is summed up quite well in this passage from the Liturgy of St. Basil the Great:

Thou didst not turn Thyself away forever from Thy creature, whom Thou hast made, O Good One, nor didst Thou forget the work of Thy hands. Through the tender compassion of Thy mercy, Thou didst visit him in various ways; Thou didst send prophets; Thou didst perform mighty works by Thy Saints, who in every generation were well-pleasing unto Thee; Thou didst speak to us by the mouths of Thy servants the prophets, foretelling us of the salvation which was to come; Thou didst appoint angels as guardians. And when the fullness of time had come, Thou didst speak to us through Thy Son, Himself, by Whom Thou didst also make the ages; Who, being the radiance of Thy glory and the image of Thy person, upholding all things by the Word of His power, thought it not robbery to be equal to Thee, the God and Father. He was God before the ages, yet He appeared on earth and lived among men, becoming incarnate of a holy Virgin. He emptied Himself, taking the form of a servant, being likened to the body of our lowliness, that He might liken us to the image of His glory.

Reflection

1. What do Christians believe about Jesus that Jews and Moslems do not?

2. What did St. Peter affirm about Christ?

3. What does Jesus have to do with the history of Israel?

4. Why did most of the Jews of Jesus' day not recognize Him as the Messiah?

5. What is Jesus' relation to God?

6. Did Jesus have a human father? What does this say about Him?

7. What did the Incarnation accomplish for the salvation of mankind?

8. How has Christ restored the image of God in man?

9. In what way has humanity been joined to the divine nature?

10. Did Jesus ever commit a sin? What does this have to do with our salvation?

CHAPTER FOUR

The Death
and Resurrection
of Christ

*Today He Who hung the earth upon the waters
is hung upon the Cross.*
*He Who is King of the angels is arrayed in a
crown of thorns.*
*He Who wraps the heaven in clouds is wrapped
in the purple of mockery.*
*He Who in Jordan set Adam free receives blows
upon His face.*
*The Bridegroom of the Church is transfixed
with nails.*
The Son of the Virgin is pierced with a spear.
We venerate Thy Passion, O Christ.
Show us also Thy glorious Resurrection.[1]

Thus far, we have seen that the Only-begotten Son
of God became man for our sake, taking upon Himself
our human nature. It was not enough for our salvation,
however, that He simply come and live on earth as a
man. He had to assume every aspect of human exis-

---

[1] *The Lenten Triodion,* tr. by Mother Mary and K. Ware (London: Faber and Faber, 1978), p. 609.

tence, for as St. Gregory the Theologian said, "What is not assumed is not healed." This means that in order to free us from the bondage of sin and death and give us His eternal life, Christ had to share in our death as well as in our life.

Let us briefly review what we have already said about death. On the one hand, as a biological phenomenon, death is perfectly natural. But on the other hand, as persons created in the image of God, we were made for more than mere biological life. Through our own self-centeredness, however, we have estranged ourselves from the One Who is life and have therefore limited ourselves to the few short years we live upon the earth. Thus, death is the ultimate reality that faces every single one of us. St. John of Damascus, in one of his funeral hymns, expresses the tragedy and horror of death:

To what can our life be likened? Truly unto a flower, a mist, and the dew of the morning. Come, therefore, let us gaze keenly at the grave. Where is the beauty of the body, and where is its youth? Where are the eyes and the fleshly form? Like the grass all have perished, all have been destroyed.

... Come, O brethren, let us gaze into the grave upon the dust and ashes from which we were made. Where do we go now? What are we to become? Who is poor, who rich? Who is the master, who the freeman? Are not we all ashes? The beauty of the countenance is moldered, and

death has withered up all the flower of youth
... Truly all mortal things are vanity.

The Son of God became man not only in order to teach us about God and to show us how to live, but to enter into the lowest depth of human existence—death itself—in order to raise us up to eternal life in His Heavenly Kingdom. The Gospels recount for us the story of Jesus' last hours. After eating His final meal with His disciples (the Last Supper), Jesus was betrayed by one of His followers, Judas Iscariot. He was arrested in the Garden of Gethsemane, where He had gone to pray. He was taken before the religious authorities and was accused of blasphemy because He claimed to be the Son of God. They, in turn, sent Him to the Roman Governor, Pontius Pilate, and accused Him of inciting a rebellion against Caesar. When Pilate offered to free Christ, the crowd instead asked for Barabbas, a hardened criminal. Thus, Jesus was crucified by the Romans at the urging of the religious authorities of Jerusalem.

After dying upon the cross, He was buried in the private tomb of one of His followers, Joseph of Arimathea. The next Sunday morning, however, when Jesus' women disciples went to the tomb to complete the burial preparations, they found that it was empty. An angel told them that Jesus had risen from the dead. Later on, they and the other disciples encountered Christ Himself and knew that He was alive (cf. Matthew 26:17-28:20).

In Jesus Christ, God not only became man, He took upon Himself the worst consequences of our disobedience—death. We must remember that He did all of this freely, not because He had to. Jesus said that no man had the power to take His life, but that He laid down His life of His own accord (John 10:18). The fact that Jesus was unjustly accused and executed underscores the fact that for Him death itself was unjust, for He alone was without sin. He alone lived in perfect communion with the Father. Yet, He accepted to be born as a man in a world filled with hatred and evil, to be mistreated and hated by those He came to save, and to die on the cross as a common criminal so that through His death we might have life. Consider these words from the prophet Isaiah:

> *Surely He hath borne our griefs, and carried our sorrows: yet we did esteem Him stricken, smitten of God, and afflicted. But He was wounded for our transgressions, He was bruised for our iniquities: the chastisement of our peace was upon Him; and with His stripes we are healed. All we like sheep have gone astray; we have turned every one to his own way; and the LORD hath laid on Him the iniquity of us all* (Isaiah 53:4-6).

By voluntarily becoming man, living a perfect human life, dying on the cross, and rising again, Jesus Christ opens the way for all of us to return to the house of the Father and to share in God's eternal life. Consider the words of St. Mark the Ascetic:

> When we were in this harsh captivity, ruled by invisible and bitter death, the Master of all visible and invisible creation was not ashamed to humble Himself and to take upon Himself our

human nature, subject as it was to the passions
of shame and desire and condemned by divine
judgment; and He became like us in all things
except that He was without sin (cf. Heb 4:15),
that is, without ignoble passions. All the penal-
ties imposed by divine judgment upon man for
the sin of the first transgression—death, toil,
hunger, thirst and the like—He took upon
Himself, become what we are, so that we might
become what He is. The Logos became man, so
that man might become what He is. The Logos
became man, so that man might become Logos.
Being rich, He become poor for our sakes, so
that through His poverty we might become rich
(cf. 2 Cor. 8:9). In His great love for man He became like us, so that through every virtue we
might become like Him.[2]

Specifically, there are three things which Jesus'
death and resurrection have accomplished for us and
for our salvation: 1) the forgiveness of sins and reconciliation with the Father, 2) freedom from the bondage
of death, and 3) the promise of the transfiguration of
the entire universe.

The Forgiveness of Sins

First of all, the writers of the New Testament and
the teachers of the Church never ceased to delight in

[2] "Letter to Nicholas the Solitary" in *The Philokalia*, Vol. 1, p.
155.

contrasting the obedience of Christ with the disobedience of Adam. Consider this passage from St. Irenaeus:

The sin which came by the tree (cf. Gen.3:6) was undone by the tree of obedience to God when the Son of man was nailed to the tree. There He overcame the knowledge of evil and brought I the knowledge of good. Evil is disobedience to God, and good is obedience to God.[3]

Indeed, this contrast is the key to understanding how Jesus' death can grant us the forgiveness of sins and reunite us with God. If our disobedience is the ultimate act of self-centeredness, Christ's voluntary death on the cross is the ultimate act of selflessness. For One Who is immortal by nature to endure mortal death is the greatest act of self-denial and self-giving. Jesus said that the greatest love one could have is to lay down one's life for one's friend. Such is the love that Jesus Christ has for each of us. Consider, then, the great contrast between Adam and Christ. Adam, a creature made from the dust of the earth, wanted to make himself into a god, but Christ...

Who, being in the form of God, thought it not robbery to be equal with God: But made Himself of no reputation, and took upon Him the form of a servant, and was made in the likeness of men: And being found in fashion as a man, He humbled Himself, and became obedient unto death, even the death of

[3] *The Preaching of the Apostles* 33, tr. by Jack N. Sparks (Brookline, MA: Holy Cross Press, 1987), p.48.

the cross. Wherefore God also hath highly exalted Him, and given Him a name which is above every name: That at the name of Jesus every knee should bow, of things in heaven, and things in earth, and things under the earth; And that every tongue should confess that Jesus Christ is Lord, to the glory of God the Father (Philippians 2:6-11).

Jesus' life of complete self-sacrifice, even to the point of dying a criminal's death, has the power to destroy the pride and self-centeredness that wrecks our lives. Through His self-sacrifice on the cross, we can receive forgiveness for our sins and the power to overcome the temptations which plague us, *For in that He Himself hath suffered, being tempted, He is able to aid them that are tempted* (Hebrews 2:18). Through His absolute obedience to God the Father, Jesus destroyed the wall of sin and pride that separates us from God and reunites us with our Creator.

Freedom from the Bondage of Death

However, Jesus has not only destroyed the power of sin and opened the way for us to return to the Father's house, He has also destroyed the chains of death that hold all men captive. The Apostle Peter preached to the people of Jerusalem:

Ye men of Israel, hear these words; Jesus of Nazareth, a man approved of God among you by miracles and wonders and signs, which God did by Him in the midst of you, as ye yourselves also know: Him, being delivered by the determinate counsel and foreknowledge of God, ye have taken, and by wicked hands have crucified and slain: Whom God hath raised up, having loosed the pains of death: because it was not possible that He should be held by it (Acts 2:22-24).

Because Jesus Christ is the Son of God, it was impossible for death to hold Him. St. Basil the Great wrote, "Descending through the cross into hell—that He might fill all things with Himself—He loosed the pangs of death. He arose on the third day, having made for all flesh a path to the resurrection from the dead, since it was not possible for the Author of Life to be a victim of corruption." Church writers often use the imagery of death as a strong prison that holds mankind captive. Jesus frees us from our captivity to death by entering into death itself, filling the realm of death with His immortal life:

Forasmuch then as the children are partakers of flesh and blood, He also Himself likewise took part of the same; that through death He might destroy him that had the power of death, that is, the devil; And deliver them who through fear of death were all their lifetime subject to bondage (Hebrews 2:14-15).

Compare this hymn from Holy Saturday:

Today hades groans and cries aloud: "My dominion has been swallowed up; the Shepherd has been crucified and he has raised Adam. I am deprived of those whom once I ruled; in my strength I devoured them, but now I have cast them forth. He Who was crucified has emptied the tombs; the power of death has no more strength." Glory to Thy Cross, O Lord, and to thy Resurrection![4]

By dying and rising again, Jesus has removed the sting of death. To be sure, people continue to die, but because Jesus Christ has filled the realm of death with His life, death is no longer the end of human existence; it becomes a passage into the immortal life of God. Jesus' resurrection from the dead is our promise that one day all people will rise from the dead and share in God's eternal life:

Behold, I show you a mystery; We shall not all sleep, but we shall all be changed, In a moment, in the twinkling of an eye, at the last trump: for the trumpet shall sound, and the dead shall be raised incorruptible, and we shall be changed. For this corruptible must put on incorruption, and this mortal must put on immortality. So when this corruptible shall have put on incorruption, and this mortal shall have put on immortality, then shall be brought to pass the saying that is written, Death is swallowed up in victory. O death, where is thy sting? O grave, where is thy victory? The sting of death is sin; and the strength of sin is the law. But thanks be to God, Who giveth us the victory through our Lord Jesus Christ (1 Corinthians 15:51-57).

At midnight on Easter throughout the world Orthodox Christians greet one another with the exclama-

---

[4] *The Lenten Triodion*, p. 656.

tion, "Christ is Risen!" "Indeed, He is risen!" This is our solemn affirmation that Jesus Christ has destroyed the power of sin and death that has held us captive. He has literally filled the realm of death with life. Those who truly trust in Jesus Christ and who have learned to share in His eternal life here and now have no need to fear physical death. We can say along with the Apostle Paul,

For whether we live, we live unto the Lord; and whether we die, we die unto the Lord: whether we live therefore, or die, we are the Lord's. For to this end Christ both died, and rose, and revived, that He might be Lord both of the dead and living (Romans 14:8-9).

One day, we shall all die, for *it is appointed unto men once to die, but after this the judgment* (Hebrews 9:27). Yet, we know that the sting of death has been removed through Christ's resurrection. Orthodox Christians, therefore, face death with the security that

neither death nor life, nor angels nor principalities nor powers, nor things present nor things to come, nor height nor depth, nor any other creature, shall be able to separate us from the love of God which is in Christ Jesus Our Lord (Romans 8:38-39).

The Transfiguration of the Universe

The life that God grants to the world through the resurrection of Christ is not limited to human beings, however. The death and resurrection of Christ also prefigures the transfiguration of the entire created order.

The women who went to Jesus' tomb early on Sunday morning to anoint His body found that His tomb was empty; His body was not there. Yet, on several occasions when the risen Lord appeared to the women and to His other disciples they did not immediately recognize Him. This fact tells us two very important things about the resurrection of Christ and about the life He grants to the world.

First of all, it tells us that Christ arose in His body. Some people believe that man is essentially an immaterial soul or spirit imprisoned in a body. But we have already seen that man was originally created not only for an eternal relationship of love with God, but also with the entire created order. God created man as a *physical* being in a *physical* world. The spiritual aspect of man's existence cannot really be separated from the physical. Therefore, for God to save man and to give him the possibility to live life as God originally intended, He must save the material world as well. The risen Christ is not a ghost or disembodied soul. Jesus Christ arose in the flesh so that the entire physical universe would share in the unending life of God.

At the same time, however, we must not think that the risen Christ was simply a reanimated corpse in the sense of someone who dies on the operating table and is brought back to life. The second thing that Jesus' resurrection tells us about the life to come is that it is a transfigured life. Jesus' resurrected body was transfigured by the glory of God. To use the words of the Apostle Paul, it had *put on immortality*. That is why the disciples did not recognize Jesus at first. When Jesus returns in glory to judge all people according to their works and to abolish even physical death, the entire created cosmos will be filled with the presence and life and glory of God—and so will all who trust in Him and willingly share in His life. *Beloved, now are we the sons of God; and it doth not yet appear what we shall be: but we know that when He shall appear, we shall be like Him, for we shall see Him as He is* (1 John 3:2).

The Old Testament book The Song of Songs speaks of love that is as strong as death. This is, in the deepest sense, the meaning of Christ's death and resurrection. His is a love so powerful, that it has overcome pride, selfishness, and even death itself. The meaning of Christ's death and resurrection is beautifully summed up in this Easter sermon by St. Gregory the Theologian, who lived during the fourth century. It expresses not only thanksgiving for what Christ has already done for us, but also the joyful hope of the life that is to come:

> Yesterday I was crucified with Him; today I am glorified with Him. Yesterday I died with Him; today I am made alive with Him. Yesterday I was buried with Him; today I am raised up with Him. Let us offer to Him Who suffered and rose again for us ... ourselves, the possession most precious to God and most proper. Let us become like Christ, since He became like us. Let us become divine for His sake, since for us He became man. He assumed the worse that He might give us the better. He became poor that by His poverty we might become rich. He accepted the form of a servant that we might win

back our freedom. He came down that we might be lifted up. He was tempted that through Him we might conquer. He was dishonored that He might glorify us. He died that He might save us. He ascended that He might draw us, who were thrown down through the fall of sin, to Himself. Let us give all, offer all, to Him Who gave Himself as a ransom and reconciliation for us. We needed an incarnate God, a God put to death, that we might live. We were put to death together with Him that we might be cleansed. We rose again with Him because we were put to death with Him. We were glorified with Him because we rose again with Him. A few drops of blood recreate the whole universe!

Reflection

1. Why did St. Gregory say "What is not assumed is not healed"?

2. Why was it necessary for Christ to assume our mortality as well as our life?

3. Why is death a tragedy for man?

4. Did Jesus have to die?

5. How does Isaiah's prophecy of the "Suffering Servant" relate to Christ?

6. How does Christ's obedience heal man's disobedience?

7. Why was death not able to hold Christ captive?

8. How is this truth expressed in the services of Holy Saturday?

9. What does the resurrection of Christ mean for us?

10. What implications does this have for the entire created universe?

CHAPTER FIVE

The Judgment, Heaven, and Hell

God is the sun of justice, as it is written, who shines rays of goodness on simply everyone. The soul develops according to its free will into either wax because of its love for God or into mud because of its love of matter. Thus just as by nature the mud is dried out by the sun and the wax is automatically softened, so also every soul which loves matter and the world and has fixed its mind far from God is hardened as mud according to its free will and by itslef advances to its perdition, as did Pharoah. However, every soul which loves God is softened as wax, and receiving divine impressions and characters it becomes the dwelling place of God in the Spirit (Eph. 2:22).[1]

We have said that through the death and resurrection of Christ God has filled the realm of death with Himself and has renewed our human nature, so that when Christ returns in glory all people will be raised from the dead and will share in God's eternal life. Yet, we have also said that it is only those people who fol-

---

[1] Maximus the Confessor, *Chapters on Knowledge* I:12.

THE JUDGMENT, HEAVEN AND HELL

low Christ who have no need to fear death. It is only those who participate in Christ's life *here* and *now* who will be able to enjoy the life of the Kingdom of God to come. How can this be? St. Nicholas Cabasilas, a great teacher of the Church who lived during the fourteenth century, explains that while all people will share in God's eternal life, not all people will have the capacity to *enjoy* that life:

> The resurrection is the restoration of our human nature. Such things God gives freely, for just as He forms us without us willing it, so He forms us anew though we have contributed nothing to it. On the other hand, the Kingdom and vision of God and union with Christ are privileges which depend on willingness. They are thus possible only for those who have been willing to receive them and have loved them and longed for them. For such it is fitting that they should enjoy the presence of the things for which they longed; for the unwilling it is impossible.... Like a blind man he would fall out of this life into that, bereft of every sense and faculty by which it is possible to know and love the Savior and to wish to be united to Him and to be able to achieve it. One need not therefore marvel that while all will live in immortality, it is not all who will live in blessedness. All equally enjoy God's providence for our nature, but it is only those who are devout towards

God who enjoy the gifts which adorn their willingness.[2]

The Judgment

Jesus said that when He shall come again with all the hosts of heaven He shall sit upon the throne of His glory *and before Him shall be gathered all nations: and He shall separate them one from another, as a shepherd divideth his sheep from the goats* (Matthew 25:31-32). One day we will all stand before the judgment of God. It is significant that we will be judged by Jesus Christ and not by God the Father, for it was the Son of God Who became man for us and lived a perfect human life (John 5:27). On that day we will stand before the One Who lived a perfect human life in complete love and obedience and Who gave His own life for the salvation of others. His very presence will be a great judgment, for all of our deepest desires and motives will be brought to light as well as all of our deeds. We will be called to give an account for every idle word we have spoken (cf. Matthew 12:36).

On that day the innermost treasure of our hearts will be revealed, *for out of the abundance of the heart the mouth speaketh. A good man out of the good treasure of the heart bringeth forth good things, and an evil man out of the evil treasure bringeth forth evil things* (Matthew 12:34-35). In the end we will all be given that which we desire most in our heart of hearts when God...

[2]Nicholas Cabasilas, *The Life in Christ* (Crestwood: SVS Press, 1974), pp. 81-82.

will render to every man according to his deeds: To
them who by patient continuance in well doing seek
for glory and honor and immortality, eternal life:
But unto them that are contentious, and do not obey
the truth, but obey unrighteousness, indignation
and wrath . . . (Romans 2:6-8)

Thus, how we live in the life to come depends on
how we live in this life. If in our deepest heart we love
God and seek His Kingdom, we shall surely find it. But
if we are wrapped up in ourselves instead, we shall be
unable to enjoy the life that God grants freely to all.
Metropolitan Anthony Bloom, a Russian bishop now
living in London, gives us an especially helpful analogy: "Have you ever noticed that to be rich means an
impoverishment on another level? It is enough for you
to say, 'I have this watch, it is mine,' and to close your
hand on it, to be in possession of a watch and to have
lost a hand."[3] In other words, if we spend our life trying
to hold onto the things of this world, we will not be able
to open our arms and receive the Kingdom of God.

Judgment does not mean that God loves some people and hates others, or that God takes delight in the
punishment of sinners. God loves all people equally
and desires that all share in His life of love, yet there are
some people who by the selfish disposition of their own
hearts render themselves incapable of receiving and responding to God's love. When we stand before Christ
on the Day of Judgment, the true and eternal disposi-

[3]Anthony Bloom, *Beginning to Pray* (New York: Paulist
Press,), p. 41.

59

tion of our heart will be revealed; there will be no more
opportunity for change or repentance.

However, when we think of judgment we are often
inclined to compare ourselves to people we consider to
be worse than ourselves. We comfort ourselves with the
thought that while we may not be perfect, we are not as
bad as people like Hitler. Yet most of the trouble in the
world is caused by ordinary people like us. Few people
set out in life with the goal of becoming evil. It is the
little things–petty jealousies and grievances–which act
as cancerous cells within the heart. Unless we are prepared to take drastic action–to seek the help of the
Great Physician Who can replace these cells with His
love and mercy–then eventually our heart will be
overcome with the cancer of selfishness. St. John of
Kronstadt, a Russian priest noted for his great wisdom
and spiritual power, reveals how the cancer of sin
spreads throughout our life:

> The root of every evil is a self-loving heart, or
> self-pity, self-sparing; it is from self-love, or ex-
> cessive and unlawful love for oneself that all
> the vices proceed.... Sins of thought are not an
> unimportant matter for the Christian, because
> all that is pleasing to God in us is comprised in
> thoughts, for the thoughts are the beginning
> from which words and deeds proceed. Words
> are important because they either benefit those
> who hear them, or are corrupt and tempt oth-
> ers, perverting their hearts and thoughts; deeds
> still more so, because examples act more pow-
> erfully than anything upon people, inciting

them to imitate them. The Lord is so holy, so simple in His holiness, that one single evil or impure thought deprives us of Him, Who is the peace and light of our souls.[4]

Likewise, Archimandrite Sophrony, the disciple of St. Silouan of Mt. Athos, explains how even the smallest sin has cosmic consequences:

> The essence of sin consists not in the infringement of ethical standards but in a falling away from the divine eternal life for which man was made and to which, by his very nature, he is called. Sin is committed first of all in the secret depths of the human spirit, but its consequences distort the whole individual. A sin will reflect on a man's psychological and physical condition, on his outward appearance, on his personal destiny. Sin will, inevitably, pass beyond the boundaries of the sinner's own life to burden all humanity and thus affect the fate of the whole world. The sin of our forefather Adam was not the only sin of cosmic significance. Every sin, secret and manifest, committed by each one of us, has a bearing on the rest of the universe.[5]

Unless the love of God reigns in our heart, selfishness and pride will reign there. Have you ever known

---

[4]Fr. John of Kronstadt, *Spiritual Counsels* (Crestwood: SVS Press, 1989), p. 111.

[5]Archimandrite Sophrony, *The Monk of Mt. Athos* (Crestwood: SVS Press, 1975), p. 22.

someone who is completely wrapped up in his or her own selfishness and bitterness? Such a person can never be pleased. Others are always a fault. Even though such a person may never have done anything really "bad", his or her bitterness becomes positively infectious and affects the lives of others. This is an example of what can happen to each of us if we allow the cancerous cells of selfishness and pride to grow within us. The inner disposition of our heart will determine not only how we will fare in our old age in *this* life, but more importantly, how we shall fare in the life to come:

> The degrees of bliss and torment in the next world will vary. This is proved by the present state of the souls of different people, or of the same man at different times, in different circumstances. The simpler, the better and more unselfish a man is, the more blessed he is inwardly; the more dishonest, selfish and evil he is, the more unhappy; the firmer his faith and the stronger his love, the more blessed he is; the weaker his faith and love, the weaker he feels. Thus, those who have little or no faith, those who hate their fellows, are the most unhappy of men. By this we can understand what future torments will be, and future bliss.[6]

Thus, the innermost depth of our heart is a battleground. We see the effects of sin every time we turn on the television or read a newspaper. You yourself know the effect which sin can have in your own life. Are you

[6]Fr. John of Kronstadt, p. 230.

willing to come to the One Who has the power to deliver you from the bondage of pride and selfishness? Are you willing to place your life in the hands of the One Who has the power to deliver you from the living death of sin and give you the unending life of God? Jesus Christ is waiting to lead you back to the house of the Father. By turning to Him in faith, you can know the peace and love of God. *Come to Me, all you who labor and are heavy laden, and I will give you rest* (Matthew 11:28).

Heaven and Hell

Ultimately, our eternal destiny hinges on what we really *want.* Jesus warned us not to store up for ourselves treasure on earth. One day all of the things for which people work so hard will be gone. There is a great deal of truth to the saying, "You can't take it with you." Things that are so important in this world — money, power, status–will be meaningless in the world to come. That is why Jesus counseled us to store up for ourselves treasure in heaven. The Kingdom to come consists of love, goodness, mercy, kindness, peace, and self-giving (cf. Romans 14:17). Only those who love and treasure these things will be able to enjoy eternal life with God.

In the Sermon on the Mount, Jesus gave us a stern warning: *Where your treasure is, there will your heart be also* (Matthew 6:21). What we really desire in life reflects the true disposition of our heart — the innermost core of our being. If we are to know joy and blessedness in the Kingdom of God, the journey must begin in our heart.

The Psalmist wrote, *Blessed are those in whose hearts are the highways to Zion* (Psalm 84:5). Jesus Himself said, *The Kingdom of God is within you* (Luke 17:21). Through the decisions that we make day by day that show the disposition of our heart, we are either moving closer to the Kingdom of God or further away from it. Thus, the innermost desires of our heart will either lead us to Heaven or to hell.

Now most of us are accustomed to thinking of hell as some sort of cosmic furnace. However, we must not think of hell so much as a "place" where bad people are sent to be punished, but rather as the opposite of the Kingdom of heaven. If the joyous life of the Kingdom of God begins in the human heart, then it must also be true that hell begins there as well. Where love and self-giving do not reign in the human heart, selfishness and pride will.

The great, Russian novelist Dostoevsky wrote that Hell "is the suffering of being no longer able to love.... And yet it is impossible to take this spiritual torment from them, for this torment is not external but is within them."[7] Dostoevsky stresses the fact that it is the inner disposition of our heart that will determine our eternal destiny. If in our heart of hearts we love God and give of ourselves and earnestly seek peace and goodness, then we will be able to enjoy the blessedness of life with God. But, on the other hand, if we close off our hearts in

---

[7]Fyodor Dostoevsky, *The Brothers Karamazov*, Tr. by Richard Pevear and Larissa Volokhonsky (New York: Vintage Classics, 1991), pp. 322-323.

selfishness and pride, we imprison ourselves in a hell of our own making.

Hell is not an external punishment imposed on us by an angry God; it is our own inability to live the life of love which God intends for us. Cabasilas explains this fact by comparing the ability to enjoy the Kingdom of God to our sensory organs:

> The Life in Christ originates in this life and arises from it. It is perfected, however, in the life to come, when we shall have reached that last day. It cannot attain perfection in men's souls in this life, nor even in that which is to come, without already having begun here.... But if the life to come were to admit those who lack the faculties and senses necessary for it, it would avail nothing for their happiness, but they would be dead and miserable living in that blessed and immortal world. The reason is, that the light would appear and the sun shine with its pure rays with no eye having been formed to see it. The Spirit's fragrance would be abundantly diffused and pervading all, but one would not know it without already having the sense of smell.[8]

You see, then, heaven and hell are primarily *subjective* experiences. God is not an egotistical tyrant. He does not get angry — contrary to the sermon, "Sinners in the Hands of an Angry God," that you no doubt read in high school. Nor does He live according to some exter-

8Cabasilas, p. 43.

nal code of justice whereby He is constrained to punish sinners. *God is love* (1 John 4:8): this is not a description of God but a definition. God acts always and toward every creature with love, bestowing the fullness of His goodness on all: *for He maketh His sun to rise on the evil and on the good, and sendeth rain on the just and on the unjust* (Mat. 5:45). What separates the just and the unjust is their ability to receive God's love. As St. Maximus said in the quotation with which we began this chapter, the sun is one and the same; it is the receptivity of the subject that makes it malleable and therefore capable of receiving the divine imprint (like wax) or hard and cracked (like dried mud).

St. Isaac the Syrian said that the fire of hell is the love of God.[9] St. Paul wrote, *For our God is a consuming fire* (Heb. 12:29), and, *It is a fearful thing to fall into the hands of the living God* (Heb 10:31). Those who are able to receive the love of God experience His presence as light and joy. This fire, which is not material, but the grace of God, purifies the soul and makes us like Christ: *Beloved, now are we the sons of God, and it doth not yet appear what we shall be: but we know that, when He shall appear, we shall be like Him; for we shall see Him as He is* (1 John 3:2). On the other hand, those who, through the enslavement to their passions, are incapable of receiving and responding to the love of God will experience God's presence and love as condemnation:

---

[9] *Ascetical Homilies* 28. St. Isaac defines Paradise in the same way.

These things mean that men's experiences of god will be different. "To each by himself the Master will give according to the measure of his excellence and his worthiness" (St. Isaac). For there the order of those who teach and those who learn will cease, and in each will be the "ardent love of all." Thus there will be one who will give His grace to all, that is, God Himself, but men will receive it according to their capacity. The love of God will fall on all men, but it will act in a two-fold way, punishing the sinners and giving joy to the righteous. St. Isaac the Syrian, expressing the Orthodox Tradition on this subject, writes: "The power of love works in two ways: it torments sinners, even as happens here when a friend suffers from a friend; but it becomes a source of joy for those who have observed its duties." Therefore the same love of God, the same energy will fall upon all men, but it will work differently.[10]

Does this mean that there will be no "physical" separation between the saints and sinners in eternity? No. There will surely be separation, if only for the sake of the elect, for the Scripture says that there will be no sorrow there (cf. Rev. 21:4). The point is, however, that while the sinners may be separated from the saints, Christ will be everywhere: *And when all things shall be*

[10] Hierotheos Vlachos, *Life After Death*, tr. by Esther Williams (Levadia, Greece: Birth of the Theotokos Monastery, 1995), pp. 255-256.

subdued unto Him, then shall the Son also Himself be subject unto Him that put all things under Him, that God may be all in all (1 Cor. 15:28). There will be no place to hide from the presence of Christ. It is His presence that will be heaven or hell.

Reflection

1. Will all people rise from the dead when Christ returns?

2. Will all enjoy the blessedness of the Kingdom of Heaven?

3. Who will judge us on the Day of Judgment?

4. By what criteria will we be judged?

5. Does God hate sinners?

6. Are there such things as small sins?

7. How will the way we live affect our future destiny?

8. What is the nature of hell?

9. Why does God not destroy sinners altogether?

10. In the final analysis, what will determine our eternal destiny?

CHAPTER SIX

Union with Christ

You cannot have God for your Father if you have not the Church for your mother. If there was escape outside the ark of Noah, there is escape too for one who is found to be outside the Church. Our Lord warns us when He says: "He that is not with me is against me, and he that gathereth not with me, scattereth" (Mat. 12:30).[1]

So far, we have discussed what God has done for the salvation of mankind. The Second Person of the Trinity — the eternal Son and Word of God — assumed human nature in its entirety, being born of the Virgin Mary. Through His life, death, resurrection, and ascension to Heaven, He has healed the consequences of man's sin and opened the way once more for man to attain the purpose for which he was created: participation in the unending life of God Himself. Thus, Christ has *already saved* humankind. We have also seen, however, that while all people will rise from the dead, not all will experience the presence of Christ as life and blessing. The difference between heaven and hell, as we have already said, is ultimately *subjective* or, to be as

---

[1] St. Cyprian of Carthage, *On the Unity of the Catholic Church* 6.

specific as possible, *personal*. This brings us to the subject of what *we* must do to attain salvation.

Faith

In what is without doubt the best-known verse in the New Testament, St. John writes, *For God so loved the world, that he gave his only begotten Son, that whosoever believeth in him should not perish, but have everlasting life* (John 3:16).[2] Belief—faith—is the starting point for man's salvation, for, as St. Paul says, *But without faith it is impossible to please Him: for he that cometh to God must believe that He is, and that He is a rewarder of them that diligently seek Him* (Heb. 11:6).[3]

What is faith? St. Paul answers this question:

Now faith is the substance of things hoped for, the evidence of things not seen.... Through faith we understand that the worlds were framed by the word of God, so that things which are seen were not made of things which do appear (Heb 11:1, 3).

We said earlier that one of the effects of the fall of man is the fact that we no longer see creation as it really is. *The heavens declare the glory of God; and the firmament*

[2] From the syntax of the passage, it is difficult to tell whether these are the words of Christ or St. John's own commentary. In either case, this verse represents the single best one-sentence summation of the Gospel in the Bible.

[3] The attribution of the Book of Hebrews is traditional. However, it was questioned even in the early Church. Whether it was written by St. Paul himself or one of his close disciples, the Church has accepted Hebrews as an authentic witness to the Gospel and, therefore, truly Holy Scripture.

showeth His handiwork (Psa. 18[19]:1). Yet, we do not see this because our understanding has been darkened by the passions. To see the world as it truly is — as the showplace of God's creative activity — we must see with the eyes of faith. Faith is *the evidence of things not seen.*

Notice in this passage that St. Paul explicitly links faith with the understanding that God created the world and that God created it out of nothing. Faith is necessary if we are to understand by whom — and why — the world was created.[4]

All of this is not to suggest, however, that faith must necessarily be "blind." On the contrary, faith in the Orthodox tradition is rooted in experience. Toward the end of his Gospel, St. John wrote, *And he that saw it bare record, and his record is true: and he knoweth that he saith true, that ye might believe* (John 19:35). And again, *But these are written, that ye might believe that Jesus is the*

---

[4] I have written elsewhere on the subject of Evolution and Creation (*The Faith*, pp. 75-79). I am firmly convinced that evolutionary theory is poor science, poor philosophy, and even worse theology. However, "creationism" is not provable scientifically. Nor, is it possible to "prove" the existence of God. This does not mean that belief in God is irrational. If anything, it is evolutionary theory that is irrational. But it does mean that God is beyond the categories of human reason — as He is beyond all created categories of Being and Understanding. God cannot be apprehended by the human mind; He must be seen and known through the eyes of faith. Belief in God and in His creation of the world from nothing is certainly *reasonable* — surely more reasonable than the belief that life in all of its complexity is the result of a series of self-actualizing accidents. But, it is not logically *provable*, as if God were one more object among many in the creation that we can analyze and squeeze into neat syllogisms.

Christ, the Son of God; and that believing ye might have life through His name (John 20:31).

The Bible is not a set of oracles, dictated by God, but a set of witnesses to what God has done in history. This is quite a different conception of Scripture than that held by many other religions. Moslems, for example, believe that the Koran was dictated to Mohamed directly by God and that the Book is literally the Word of God.[5] It is amazing how similar the Moslem view of Scripture is to that of modern evangelical and fundamentalist Protestants.[6] In short, the Word of God is a book.

For the Orthodox, however, the Word of God is not a book, but a person, the Second Person of the Trinity, the eternal Son of God the Father. The Bible is the written testimony of those who have *experienced* the presence of the Word of God among men. To quote St. John again:

That which was from the beginning, which we have heard, which we have seen with our eyes, which we

---

[5] This implies — and this is Islamic doctrine — that the Word of God is, and can only be, in Arabic. A pious Moslem is expected to learn Arabic so that he can read the Word of God. English and other translations are not called translations, but "interpretations." Technically, the Koran cannot be translated.

[6] Baptists pride themselves on calling themselves "People of the Book," yet few if any realize that this phrase was first bestowed on Christians by Moslems. In the Islamic kingdoms, Christians and Jews were given privileges above those of mere pagans because they were "People of the Book." No doubt the Moslems simply assumed that Christians regarded the Bible in the same way that Moslems regarded the Koran.

have looked upon, and our hands have handled, of the Word of life; (For the life was manifested, and we have seen it, and bear witness, and show unto you that eternal life, which was with the Father, and was manifested unto us;) That which we have seen and heard declare we unto you, that ye also may have fellowship with us: and truly our fellowship is with the Father, and with His Son Jesus Christ (1 John 1:1-3).

Thus, for the Orthodox, faith is not a blind leap into irrationality, but an act of trust based upon the testimony of others that God is and that He loves His creation. Furthermore, these testimonies are not limited to those who lived in biblical times. Since the day of Pentecost, when the Church was born, there have been holy men and women who have truly known the risen Christ and have been transformed by Him into the likeness of God. Many of these people the Church has glorified as saints. This means that the Church recognizes in them the image and likeness of God, recognizes them as faithful witnesses to Christ.[7] All Christians should read the lives of the saints—particularly modern saints such as St. Nectarios, St. Elizabeth the Newmartyr, and St. John Maximovitch[8]—for these accounts confirm that Christ is truly present in His Church.

[7] It is no accident that our word, "martyr," literally means "witness" in Greek. The martyrs are precisely those who have borne witness to Christ.

[8] See the section on the Lives of Modern Saints in the bibliography at the end of this volume.

Of course, there are a lot of people out there who claim to have a special relationship with God, and they are only too happy to tell you about it. There must be some way of testing these witnesses, to see if their testimony is consistent with that of others. This is where the Bible, the creeds and conciliar decisions, and the liturgy of the Church become indispensable. These things—the Bible first and foremost—constitute the standard, the plumb line against which all other "testimonies" are measured.

St. Paul warns Timothy of the need of such a standard:

> *O Timothy, keep that which is committed to thy trust, avoiding profane and vain babblings, and oppositions of science falsely so called. Which some professing have erred concerning the faith.* (1 Tim 6:20-21).

"Orthodoxy" literally means, "right belief." Right belief is necessary for salvation because what we believe about God will determine how we relate to Him. If we have a false conception of Christ, then we will not be able to relate to Him properly and receive His healing. The goal of salvation is perfect God-likeness. But this is unattainable unless we have a right conception of God.[9] St. Paul explains this:

---

[9] This does *not* mean that we ever *understand* God, Who is beyond all of our created conceptions. Rather, it means that we do not have *false* conceptions about Him that can lead us astray. The Church's doctrinal definitions are not an attempt to describe God,

Till we all come in the unity of the faith, and of the knowledge of the Son of God, unto a perfect man, unto the measure of the stature of the fulness of Christ: That we henceforth be no more children, tossed to and fro, and carried about with every wind of doctrine, by the sleight of men, and cunning craftiness, whereby they lie in wait to deceive (Eph. 4:13-14).

Repentance

It is evident, then, that faith must be grounded in the truth. There is no merit in believing in something that is not true. On the contrary, belief in falsehood can only lead us away from Christ, Who is the *Truth*. Faith, however, is not simply an act of intellectual belief. As St. James says, the devil and his minions "believe" intellectually that God is real, but they still turn away from Him: *Thou believest that there is one God; thou doest well: the devils also believe, and tremble* (James 2:19).

Perhaps "trust" would be a better translation than faith. True faith in God is a trust in Him that leads to action. To quote St. James again, *What doth it profit, my brethren, though a man say he hath faith, and have not works? Can faith save him?* (James 2:14). Faith that remains in the head is not saving faith. Faith must move the heart and the hands and the feet. Faith is the spiritual force by which the Christian moves:

but rather to rule out false ideas and false paths that lead to destruction, rather than salvation.

I am crucified with Christ: nevertheless I live; yet not I, but Christ liveth in me: and the life which I now live in the flesh I live by the faith of the Son of God, who loved me, and gave Himself for me (Gal 2:20).

The first action that faith brings is repentance. To repent means to turn around. It means a change of mind, heart, and direction in life. The first sermon that Jesus ever preached was simply, *Repent: for the Kingdom of Heaven is at hand* (Mat. 4:17). With the fall of Adam and Eve, mankind turned itself away from God, seeking to find the meaning of existence in the created order. If we wish to find the Kingdom of God, we must "turn around" — repent — and once again direct our attention toward our Creator and Lord.

The Holy Fathers tell us that repentance is a life-long process, not a once-in-a-lifetime event. As long as we live in this world, our attention will be pulled back to creation, away from our Creator. Therefore, we must continually re-orient our lives toward God. Even those who have already been united to Christ in baptism must continually repent of their sins and redirect their attention, as St. Peter of Damaskos says:

If we so wish, however, God's second gift of grace — repentance — can lead us back to our former beauty. But if we fail to repent, inevitably we will depart with the unrepentant demons into age long punishment, more by our own free choice than against our will. Yet God did not create us for wrath but for salvation, so that we might enjoy His blessings; and we should therefore be thankful and grateful towards our Benefactor.[10]

Union with Christ in the Church

To repent does not simply mean that one feels sorry that one has sinned, though that is a beginning. To repent is to change. We cannot change, however, on our own any more than we can cure ourselves of cancer. Belief without action is, as St. Maximus says, the theology of demons (cf. James 2:19). Yet our ability to act is restricted by our lack of knowledge (what is the right thing to do?) and by our enslavement to sin (*For we know that the law is spiritual: but I am carnal, sold under sin. For that which I do I allow not: for what I would, that do I not; but what I hate, that do I* (Rom. 7:14-15). Without the Grace of God, true change is impossible.

The Son of God assumed human nature so that we might be able to share in His divine life. Only by being united to Christ and by participating in His life will we be able to live life as God intended: as a *person* living in an eternal communion of love with God, with one another, and with all of creation.

After Simon Peter confessed Jesus to be the Messiah of Israel and the Son of God, Jesus promised to build His Church and said that *the gates of hades shall not prevail against it* (Matthew 16:18). Before His death and resurrection Jesus told His disciples, *I will not leave you*

[10] *A Treasury of Divine Knowledge* Book I in *The Philokalia*, Vol. 3, p. 84.

comfortless; I will come to you (John 14:18). He promised to send them the Holy Spirit, Who would endue them with power from on high (cf. Luke 24:49). On the Day of Pentecost, fifty days after the resurrection of Christ, the Holy Spirit came upon Jesus' disciples. This was the birth of the Church.

The Church is not a social organization or a group of people with similar social or political beliefs. Rather, She is the presence and life of Christ on earth. Just as the Son of God became man when the Holy Spirit came upon the Virgin Mary, so Christ's disciples were able to share in His life when the Holy Spirit came upon them. The life of the Church is life in Christ. Her life is His life. Her ministry is His ministry. Thus, the Church is not merely a place where Christians learn about God. When Jesus took upon Himself our human nature, He made it possible for us to share in His divine life. In the Church we *experience* and *participate in* the life of Christ.

The Apostle Paul often referred to the Church as the Body of Christ. Anyone who desires to follow Jesus Christ and to share in His life must be united to His Body, the Church. Just as Jesus Christ was a real man, Who lived a real human life, so His Church really exists. The Church is not a building; She is a People filled with the Holy Spirit who share in His life and bring His life to the world. By being united to Christ's Holy Orthodox Church through the mysteries (sacraments) of baptism, chrismation (confirmation), and the Holy Eucharist we share in the life of Christ. St. Nicholas Cabasilas summarizes this by commenting on the biblical verse, *For in him we live, and move, and have our being*

(Acts 17:28):

> Baptism confers being and in short, existence according to Christ. It receives us when we are dead and corrupted and first leads us to life. The anointing with chrism perfects him who has received [new] birth by infusing into him the energy that befits such a life. The Holy Eucharist preserves and continues this life and health, since the Bread of life enables us to preserve that which has been acquired and to continue in life. It is therefore by this Bread that we live and by the chrism that we are moved, once we have received being from the baptismal washing. In this way we live in God. We remove our life from this visible world to that world which is not seen by exchanging, not the place, but the very life itself and its mode.[11]

The importance of baptism is repeatedly stressed in the New Testament and by the Fathers of the Church. First of all, baptism is a new birth, our recreation in Christ. Jesus told Nicodemus, *Verily, verily, I say unto thee, Except a man be born of water and of the Spirit, he cannot enter into the Kingdom of God* (John 3:5). St. Paul adds, *For as many of you as have been baptized into Christ have put on Christ* (Gal 3:27). St. Nicholas Cabasilas explains, "To be baptized, then, is to be born according to Christ and to receive our very being and nature, having previously been nothing."[12]

---

[11] Nicholas Cabasilas, pp. 49-50.
[12] Nicholas Cabasilas, p. 66.

Baptism is also our union with Christ's death and resurrection. St. Paul stresses this point in his letter to the Church of Rome:

> *Know ye not, that so many of us as were baptized into Jesus Christ were baptized into His death? Therefore, we are buried with Him by baptism into death: that like as Christ was raised up from the dead by the glory of the Father, even so we also should walk in newness of life. For if we have been planted together in the likeness of His death, we shall be also in the likeness of His resurrection: Knowing this, that our old man is crucified with Him, that the body of sin might be destroyed, that henceforth we should not serve sin. For he that is dead is freed from sin. Now if we be dead with Christ, we believe that we shall also live with Him: Knowing that Christ being raised from the dead dieth no more; death hath no more dominion over Him. For in that He died, He died unto sin once: but in that He liveth, He liveth unto God. Likewise reckon ye also yourselves to be dead indeed unto sin, but alive unto God through Jesus Christ our Lord* (Rom. 6:5-11).

Again, consider this passage from St. Nicholas Cabasilas:

> He who seeks to be united with Him must therefore share with Him in His flesh, partake of deification, and share in His death and resurrection. So we are baptized in order that we

may die that death and rise again in that resurrection.[13]

In the mystery of chrismation, the newly illumined[14] received the "seal of the gift of the Holy Spirit." When God created the first man, *the LORD God formed man of the dust of the ground, and breathed into his nostrils the breath of life; and man became a living soul* (Gen. 2:7). So too, when we are recreated in Christ at our baptism, we receive the Holy Spirit, Who gives life according to Christ.

When Jesus was baptized by John in the Jordan River, the Holy Spirit descended upon Him in the form of a dove (cf. Mat. 3:16). This same anointing is given to Christians who "put on Christ" at their baptism. St. Cyril of Jerusalem writes:

> Having been baptized into Christ, and put on Christ, ye have been made conformable to the Son of God; for God having predestined us to the adoption of sons, made us share the fashion of Christ's glorious body. Being therefore made partakers of Christ, ye are properly called Christs, and of you God said, *Touch not my Christs* (cf. Psa. 105:15), or anointed. Now ye were made Christs, by receiving the emblem of the Holy Spirit; and all things were in a figure wrought in you, because ye are figures of

[13] Nicholas Cabasilas, pp. 65-66.

[14] Baptism is also called "Illumination" because those who were once in darkness are led into the light of Christ. Thus, the newly baptized are referred to as the newly illumined.

Christ. He also bathed Himself in the river Jordan, and having imparted the fragrance of His Godhead to the waters, he came up from them; and the Holy Spirit in substance lightened on Him, like resting up on like. In the same manner to you also, after you had come up from the pool of the sacred streams, was given the Unction, the emblem of that wherewith Christ was anointed; and this is the Holy Spirit; of Whom also the blessed Isaiah, in his prophecy respecting Him, says in the person of the Lord, *The Spirit of the Lord is upon Me, because he hath anointed me to preach glad tidings to the poor* (Isaiah 61:1).[15]

Thus, in baptism we are united with Christ and through the Holy Chrism we are anointed with the same Spirit that we might live after the likeness of Christ. Both baptism and chrismation, however, find their perfection in the Most Holy Mystery of the Table of the Lord. St. Nicholas Cabasilas writes:

After the chrismation we go to the table. This is the perfection of the life in Christ; for those who attain it there is nothing lacking for the blessedness which they seek. It is no longer death and the tomb and a participation in the better life we receive, but the risen One Himself. Nor do we receive such gifts of the Spirit as we may, but the very Benefactor Himself, the very Tem-

[15] *On the Sacraments* (*Mystagogical Catechesis* III), tr. by F. L. Cross (Crestwood, NY: SVS Press, 1986), pp. 63-64.

ple whereon is founded the whole compass of graces.... It is therefore the final Mystery as well, since it is not possible to go beyond it or to add anything to it.[16]

There is no more personal union to be had with God than that which is offered to Christians in the Holy Eucharist. This union is neither symbolic (in the modern sense of the term)[17] nor metaphorical, but actual. St. Paul writes, *The cup of blessing which we bless, is it not the communion of the blood of Christ? The bread which we break, is it not the communion of the body of Christ* (1 Cor 10:16)?

Furthermore, the Eucharist, inasmuch as it is a direct participation in the glorified humanity of Christ, is also an anticipation of the final blessedness that awaits the saints in the Kingdom of God.[18] Indeed, in the Scriptures the Kingdom is often portrayed as a great banquet (Cf. Mat. 22:2-14, Luke 22:29-30). That is why in the liturgy we "remember" the coming Kingdom as if it were already present (because it is):

Remembering, therefore, all these things that have come to pass for us, the cross, the tomb,

[16] Nicholas Cabasilas, p. 113-114.

[17] Fr. Alexander Schmemann went to great pains to distinguish the modern understanding of "symbol" from its original meaning. In modern parlance, a symbol is thought of as a sign for something *else*. Whereas, according to Fr. Schmemann, the word originally had a unitive connotation: *symbolon* unites while *diabolon* (from which we get "diabolical") sunders. See *For the Life of the World* and *The Eucharist: Sacrament of the Kingdom* (Crestwood, NY: SVS Press, 1988) p.38ff.

[18] Cf. Schmemann, *The Eucharist*, pp. 37-48.

the resurrection on the third day, the ascension into Heaven, the sitting at the Right Hand, and the Second and Glorious Coming, Thine Own of Thine Own we offer unto Thee, on behalf of all and for all.

In the Eucharist, therefore, we are truly united with Christ and enjoy, by sacramental anticipation, the blessedness of the Kingdom of God.

The Church as Our Mother

The Church is referred to as our Mother, for it is in the bosom of the Church that we are nurtured and prepared for the life of the world to come. Nicholas Cabasilas uses this imagery when he likens the life of a Christian to the development of a fetus in the womb:

As nature prepares the fetus, while it is in its dark and fluid life, for that life which is in the light, and shapes it, as though according to a model, for the life of which it is about to receive, so likewise it happens to the saint.... In this present world, therefore, it is possible for the saints not only to be disposed and prepared for that life, but also even now to live and act in accordance with it.... Yet the Lord did not promise merely to be present with the saints, but to abide with them–nay more than this, to make His abode in them.[19]

Thus, the Church is both the *preparation for* and the

[19]Nicholas Cabasilas, pp. 44-45.

experience of the life of the Kingdom of God *here* and *now.* In the Church, the relationships that have been destroyed by sin are healed and recreated. By being united to Christ, we share in His relationship of love with God the Father and are thus reunited with our Creator. *But as many as received Him, to them gave He the power to become the sons of God, even to them that believe on His name: who were born, not of blood, nor of the will of the flesh, nor of the will of man, but of God* (John 1:12-13). We are also reunited to one another in a bond that is much stronger than any physical or emotional bond, for we are united by the Holy Spirit in the one Body of Christ. *For as the body is one and hath many members, and all the members of that one body, being many, are one body, so also is Christ. For by one Spirit are we all baptized into one body— whether we be Jews or Gentiles, whether we be slaves or free— and have all been made to drink into one Spirit* (1 Corinthians 12:12-13).

Finally, our relationship with the physical world is healed as we once again learn to experience the matter of creation as a means of communion with God. *The cup of blessing which we bless, is it not the communion of the blood of Christ? The bread which we break, is it not the communion of the body of Christ? For we, being many, are one bread and one body; for we are all partakers of that one bread* (1 Corinthians 10: 16-17).

Reflection

1. What is the starting point for our salvation?

2. Is faith primarily an intellectual exercise?

3. Why do men not have faith?

4. Can the Orthodox understanding of faith be described as a "blind leap into the unknown"?

5. How is Christianity different from Islam in its understanding of Sacred Scripture?

6. What does "Orthodoxy" mean?

7. What is repentance?

8. Can man be united with Christ apart from the Church? Why or why not?

9. How do the Mysteries unite us with Christ?

10. In what way is the Church our Mother?

CHAPTER SEVEN

The Church as Spiritual Hospital

*We receive salvation by grace and as a divine
gift of the Spirit. But to attain the full measure
of virtue we need also to possess faith and love,
and to struggle to exercise our free will with in-
tegrity. In this manner we inherit eternal life as
a consequence of both grace and justice. We do
not reach the final stage of spiritual maturity
through divine power and grace alone, without
ourselves making any effort; but neither on the
other hand do we attain the final measure of
freedom and purity as a result of our own dili-
gence and strength alone, apart from divine as-
sistance. If the Lord does not build the house, it
is said, and protect the city, in vain does the
watchman keep awake, and in vain do the la-
bourer and the builder work (cf. Ps. 127:1-4).*[1]

In the Orthodox Church we often speak of grace as
the "divine energies." We must not interpret this, however, as some sort of impersonal force that operates on

---

[1] St. Symeon Metaphrastis' praphrase of the *Makarian Homilies*
I, in the *Philokalia*, Vol. 3, p. 285.

us whether we want it to or not. Grace is not electricity. Perhaps it would be better if we thought of grace in terms of medicine.

Grace as Medicine

Just as there are different kinds of medicine, so grace manifests itself in different ways. If you had a bacterial infection, you would take an antibiotic, which attacks the infection. If you had a chemical imbalance, you would take medicine that stimulates or inhibits the production of a particular chemical in your body. In short, different medicines act on the body in different ways. Now, there are not different kinds of grace as there are different medicines, but grace acts on each person in different ways, depending on the spiritual needs of each. St. Mark the Ascetic writes,

> The grace of the Spirit is one and unchanging, but energizes in each one of us as He wills. When rain falls upon the earth, it gives life to the quality inherent in each plant: sweetness in the sweet, astringency in the astringent; similarly, when grace falls upon the hearts of the faithful, it gives to each the energies appropriate to the different virtues without itself changing.[2]

The point here is that grace adapts itself to the needs and situation of the one who receives it. Thus,

---

[2] "No Righteousness by Works" 115-116, in the *Philokalia*, Vol. 1, p. 134.

grace is not only something that God gives, but also something that man must receive.

Furthermore, how we receive grace will affect how it acts in our lives, just as how we take medicine will affect how it works in our bodies. For example, certain medicines must be taken at specific times and in very specific dosages or they will not be effective. Indeed, some medicines can actually be dangerous if not taken properly. The same is true of grace.

St. Paul warns us that without the proper preparation, we dare not receive the Holy Eucharist:

> *Wherefore whosoever shall eat this bread, and drink this cup of the Lord, unworthily, shall be guilty of the body and blood of the Lord. But let a man examine himself, and so let him eat of that bread, and drink of that cup. For he that eateth and drinketh unworthily, eateth and drinketh damnation to himself, not discerning the Lord's body. For this cause many are weak and sickly among you, and many sleep* (1 Cor. 11:27-30).

To understand this, we must keep in mind what we said earlier about the presence of God. God *is* love. He always acts with love toward His creation. However, whether we experience His presence as peace and joy or as judgment and condemnation is up to *us*. Those who are properly prepared to receive the Holy Eucharist receive it as the "medicine of immortality." Those, on the other hand, who are not properly prepared, receive it in a negative way. God is fire: the saints are purified and glorified by this fire while sinners are burned by it.

The Good Physician

All of this underscores the need for proper guidance. No one—well, no one who wanted to get well—would just start taking medicine willy nilly. If, as the saying goes, a man who acts as his own lawyer in court has a fool for a client, then surely the same is true for the man who tries to diagnose and treat himself. Just as we need a doctor to diagnose and treat our physical illness, so we are in need of a true physician who can diagnose and treat our spiritual illness.

In the Gospel, our Lord gives the following parable:

A certain man went down from Jerusalem to Jericho, and fell among thieves, which stripped him of his raiment, and wounded him, and departed, leaving him half-dead. And by chance there came down a certain priest that way: and when he saw him, he passed by on the other side. And likewise a Levite, when he was at the place, came and looked on him, and passed by on the other side. But a certain Samaritan, as he journeyed, came where he was: and when he saw him, he had compassion on him, And went to him, and bound up his wounds, pouring in oil and wine, and set him on his own beast, and brought him to an inn, and took care of him. And on the morrow when he departed, he took out two pence, and gave them to the host, and said unto him, Take care of him; and whatsoever thou spendest more, when I come again, I will repay thee (Luke 10:30-35).

Metropolitan Hierotheos Vlachos explains this parable:

In the parable of the Good Samaritan the Lord showed us several truths.... Christ treated the wounded man and brought him to the inn, to the Hospital which is the Church. Here Christ is presented as a physician who heals man's illnesses, and the Church as a Hospital.[3]

Our Lord Jesus Christ is the Great Physician (cf. Luke 5:31). He brings those who are sick with sin to His Church, which is a spiritual hospital. In the Church, we not only receive the medicines we need (the holy mysteries or sacraments), but we receive the spiritual advice and training that we need so that the mysteries will be for our health and salvation and not for ill. Let us consider a few of the resources the Church makes available to those who wish to be healed.

A Well-Trained Medical Team

After the holy mysteries themselves, perhaps the most important thing that the Church-hospital provides for our salvation is trustworthy spiritual guidance. This guidance is not limited to the clergy. The bishops have the responsibility to *rightly divide the Word of truth* (2 Tim. 2:15), that is, to interpret the Scriptures and to teach the faithful. The presbyters or priests have the responsibility of daily interaction with the faithful. The parish priest is the first person we turn to for spiritual

---

[3] *Orthodox Psychotherapy: the Science of the Fathers*, tr. by Esther Williams (Levadia, Greece: Birth of the Theotokos Monastery, 1994), p. 27.

advice. But there are others in the Church, who may not be ordained clergy, to whom we can also turn for true spiritual guidance. These are people who have themselves been "cured" — or are at least far along the path of cure — and who pass on the knowledge that they have gained from experience. Usually these people are monks or nuns, but this is not necessarily the case.

While we are on the subject of spiritual fathers, we should also say something about false guides. The Orthodox Church not only provides for us trustworthy spiritual doctors, it also gives us criteria by which we can discern the good doctors from the quacks. In Orthodoxy, the spiritual father is not the same as a guru. Below are some marks of a true spiritual father as opposed to a false guide.

First of all, a true spiritual father — or mother — is one who has learned from experience. One cannot learn how to be a spiritual guide from going to seminary or from reading books.[4] One cannot lead others to the Kingdom of God unless one has himself been led there. This is why the vast majority of spiritual fathers and mothers are monastics.

Secondly, because spiritual knowledge is gained through experience, a true spiritual father is one who practices what he preaches. A spiritual guide who does not exhibit the virtues of humility, patience, and love is a false teacher. One who has not been healed of the pas-

---

[4] This is my primary criticism of Joseph Allen's book, *Inner Way: Toward a Rebirth of Eastern Christian Spiritual Direction* (Grand Rapids: Eerdmans, 1994). See my review in *Perspectives in Religious Studies* 23:1 (Spring, 1996), pp. 87-91.

sions himself — or at least is not very far along the path of healing — cannot presume to heal others.

Third, the relationship between a believer and a true spiritual director is one of freedom in Christ. A true spiritual guide is never authoritative or manipulative. Indeed, a true father never *forces* himself or his advice on anyone.

It is true that in a monastery, a novice pledges absolute obedience to his spiritual father. However, this pledge is made as an act of his free will, and the young monk is free to leave the monastery at any time. In this way, his absolute obedience is an expression of his freedom. In the world, there is a difference in the *degree* of obedience that laypeople give to their spiritual father. Laypeople are *not* expected to give absolute obedience to a spiritual father. When they ask their father for advice, they should heed it — why else would one ask for advice? — but the father has no way to impose a penalty or a sanction on the person for not following it.

Abstinence

In addition to experienced spiritual doctors, the Church-hospital also provides various therapies that help us to battle our spiritual sickness. The first of these is abstinence. In the New Testament, Christians are enjoined to abstain not only from sin, but from the very appearance of sin (cf. 1 Thess. 5:2). This is easier said than done, however. Often our desires — what the fathers call passions — have control over us. How do we break free of the control of sin in our lives?

The fathers teach us that if we cannot control what we eat, there is no way to control the other desires that so easily take over our life. Fasting is one of the ways in which we learn to take control of our lives. There are three aspects to fasting that we need to consider.

First of all, fasting is an act of obedience. In the Church, we do not fast when we feel like it. Rather, we fast according to the rules that are given us by the Church and in conjunction with the advice of our spiritual father. Fasting is not something we do to earn merits or brownie points with God. Our fasting does absolutely nothing for God. Fasting is for *our* benefit. We receive no benefit from it, however, if it is done out of a sense of pride:

> *Moreover when ye fast, be not, as the hypocrites, of a sad countenance: for they disfigure their faces, that they may appear unto men to fast. Verily I say unto you, They have their reward. But thou, when thou fastest, anoint thine head, and wash thy face; That thou appear not unto men to fast, but unto thy Father which is in secret: and thy Father, which seeth in secret, shall reward thee openly* (Mat. 6:16-18).

There are no short cuts to the Kingdom of God. As we have seen, the essence of the fall of man is pride, self-will. Until we learn obedience, we will not develop within ourselves that God-like humility that saves us:

> It is well known that obedience is the chief among the initiatory virtues, for first it displaces presumption and then it engenders humility within us. Thus it becomes, for those

95

who willingly embrace it, a door leading to the love of God.[5]

In addition to being an act of obedience, fasting is a therapy in which we learn to govern our own desires. Thus, it is a method of self-control. St. Diadochos explains:

> Those pursuing the spiritual way should train themselves to hate all uncontrolled desires until this hatred becomes habitual. With regard to self-control in eating, we must never feel loathing for any kind of food, for to do so is abominable and utterly demonic. It is emphatically not because any kind of food is bad in itself that we refrain from it. But by not eating too much or too richly we can to some extent keep in check the excitable parts of our body. In addition we can give to the poor what remains over, for this is the mark of sincere love.[6]

We should add here that abstinence applies not only to food but to any appetite. For example, a person that spends too much time watching television or playing video games or surfing the internet, may need to fast from those activities. The point is that we, as rational creatures made in the image of God, should have control over our own lives, our appetites should not have control of us.

---

[5] St. Diadochos of Photiki, "On Spiritual Knowledge" 41 in the *Philokalia*, Vol. 1, p. 265.
[6] "On Spiritual Knowledge" 43, p. 266.

A third aspect of fasting has to do with the fathers' understanding of how different foods work on the human body. There are two kinds of fasts prescribed by the Church. One is complete, or near complete, abstinence from all food for a short period of time. The other is the abstinence from certain *kinds* of foods for a specified time. Most of the Church's fasts are of the latter variety. On Wednesdays and Fridays, and during several long periods such as Great Lent, the Church prescribes a fast from eating animal products. Red meat, in particular, is thought to excite the passions. This will not come as a surprise to many modern nutritionists and certainly not to vegetarians.

In short, therefore, the Church gives us fasting guidelines as well as the advice of experienced spiritual fathers and mothers so that we might be able to gain control over our own desires. In this way, we are able to submit our will to the will of God and receive His grace into our lives.

Watchfulness

In addition to abstinence, another therapeutic tool that the Church makes available to us is watchfulness, or attentiveness. St. Hesychios the Presbyter writes:

Watchfulness is a spiritual method which, if sedulously practiced over a long period, completely frees us with God's help from impassioned thoughts, impassioned words and evil actions. It leads, in so far as this is possible, to a sure knowledge of the inapprehensible God,

97

and helps us to penetrate the divine and hidden mysteries. It enables us to fulfil every divine commandment in the Old and New Testaments and bestows upon us every blessing of the age to come.[7]

St. Hesychios goes on to say that there are four kinds of watchfulness: 1) examining every thought that approaches the mind, 2) freeing the heart from all thought so that prayer may be undistracted, 3) continually and humbly calling on the name of Jesus, and 4) constantly remembering one's own death and the judgment that awaits.[8]

The first method is guarding the entrance of the mind and heart. Evil actions do not simply spring up out of nowhere; they begin with evil thoughts. St. Philotheos of Sinai writes,

> The person who gives himself over to evil thoughts cannot keep his outer self free from sin; and if evil thoughts have not been uprooted from the heart, they are bound to manifest themselves in evil actions.[9]

It is imperative, therefore, that we guard the entrance of our mind and heart so that evil thoughts do not enter. This also means that we must guard our physical senses, so that the things we see or hear do not incite evil thoughts within us.

[7] "On Watchfulness and Holiness" 1, in the *Philokalia*, Vol. 1, p. 162.

[8] "On Watchfulness and Holiness" 14-18, pp. 164-165.

[9] "Texts on Watchfulness" 33 in the *Philokalia*, Vol. 3, p. 29.

The second method is to free the heart from all distractions so that one can focus on prayer. It is very easy to become distracted, either during the divine services or when we pray privately at home. Thoughts enter our mind—these thoughts may be evil, neutral, or even good thoughts—and distract our attention away from Christ. Ilias the Presbyter writes, "Prayer deserts you if you give attention to thoughts within and conversations without. But if you largely ignore both in order to concentrate on it, it will return to you."[10] It is necessary, therefore, that we continually gather our straying mind and re-focus it on Christ.

The third method of watchfulness is to continually call upon the name of Jesus. St. Hesychios is referring to the "Jesus Prayer," also known as the "Prayer of the Heart." In this prayer, we continually repeat a short prayer to Christ—usually, "Lord Jesus Christ, have mercy on me the sinner." This prayer may be said at all times, either vocally or mentally. St. Hesychios explains the importance of the Jesus prayer:

> To invoke Jesus continually with a sweet longing is to fill the heart in its great attentiveness with joy and tranquility. But it is Jesus Christ, the Son of God and Himself God, cause and creator of all blessings, who completely purifies the heart; for it is written: *I am God who makes peace* (cf. Isaiah 45:7).[11]

---

[10] "Gnomic Anthology II:99 in the *Philokalia*, Vol. 3, p. 45.
[11] "On Watchfulness and Holiness" 91, pp. 177-178.

The fourth method of watchfulness is the remembrance of death. This may sound very strange to us, even morbid, yet constantly reminding ourselves of our mortality and of the fact that one day we will stand before Christ is an excellent way to defend ourselves against evil thoughts and actions. Concerning this therapeutic practice St. Philotheos writes:

> Vivid mindfulness of death embraces many virtues. It begets grief; it promotes the exercise of self-control in all things; it is a reminder of hell; it is the mother of prayer and tears; it induces guarding of the heart and detachment from material things; it is the source of attentiveness and discrimination. These in their turn produce the twofold fear of God. In addition, the purging of impassioned thoughts from the heart embraces many of the Lord's commandments. The harsh hour-by-hour struggle in which so many athletes of Christ are engaged has as it s aim precisely this purging of the heart.[12]

All of these methods are essential if we are to follow the commandments of Christ, for our Lord Himself said: *The first of all the commandments is, Hear, O Israel; The Lord our God is one Lord, and thou shalt love the Lord thy God with all thy heart, and with all thy soul, and with all thy mind, and with all thy strength: this is the first commandment* (Mark 12:29-30). This can only be accomplished, however, unless we are able to guard our heart

[12] "Texts on Watchfulness" 38, p. 30.

and mind and soul, to keep them free from evil and focused on Christ our Lord.

The Parable of the Sower

I cannot emphasize strongly enough that we do not earn God's grace. Salvation, like health, is not something that *can* be earned. Grace is God's gift to man, but whether and how we receive that gift will determine our salvation. Our Lord stressed this point in a parable:

> *And he spake many things unto them in parables, saying, Behold, a sower went forth to sow; and when he sowed, some seeds fell by the way side, and the fowls came and devoured them up: Some fell upon stony places, where they had not much earth: and forthwith they sprung up, because they had no deepness of earth: And when the sun was up, they were scorched; and because they had no root, they withered away. And some fell among thorns; and the thorns sprung up, and choked them: But other fell into good ground, and brought forth fruit, some an hundredfold, some sixtyfold, some thirtyfold* (Mat. 13:3-8).

Jesus went on to explain:

> *When any one heareth the Word of the kingdom, and understandeth it not, then cometh the wicked one, and catcheth away that which was sown in his heart. This is he which received seed by the way side. But he that received the seed into stony places, the same is he that heareth the Word, and anon with joy re-*

ceiveth it; Yet hath he not root in himself, but dureth for a while: for when tribulation or persecution ariseth because of the Word, by and by he is offended. He also that received seed among the thorns is he that heareth the Word; and the care of this world, and the deceitfulness of riches, choke the Word, and he becometh unfruitful. But he that received seed into the good ground is he that heareth the Word, and understandeth it; which also beareth fruit, and bringeth forth, some an hundredfold, some sixty, some thirty (Mat. 13:19-23).

God wants all men to be saved (cf. 1 Tim. 2:4). He offers salvation to all. Yet it is up to us whether or not His grace will find fertile soil in our hearts in which to grow and bear fruit. Prayer, fasting, vigils and all of the other works that the Church prescribes are not attempts to win God's favor, but rather they are means of preparing the soil of our heart to receive and keep the grace of God. Without this work, salvation is impossible, for Christ promised salvation not simply to those hear the Word of God but to those who keep it.

Reflection

1. In what ways is grace similar to and different from medicine?

2. Is there more than one kind of grace?

3. Why, according to St. Paul, did some people die after taking communion?

4. In the parable of the Good Samaritan, Who is the Good Samaritan?

5. What does the inn in the parable represent?

6. What characteristics must a true spiritual guide have?

7. Is a spiritual father the same as a guru?

8. What is the purpose of abstinence?

9. What are the different kinds of watchfulness?

10. Do we earn the Grace of God through our ascetical efforts?

PART TWO

TOPICAL
STUDIES

CHAPTER EIGHT

The Importance of Doctrine

Every alteration in the basic creed, each subsidence in the hidden foundations of the Church "which the Lord founded upon the rock of faith," produces sooner or later cracks of division on the "surface" of the Church's face. If dogma is falsified, whether intentionally or not, ecclesiology, both pastoral and administrative, is deformed, spiritual life is falsified and man suffers.... every problem for the Church is the problem of the personal salvation of each of the faithful. Consequently, when the heretic lays hands on the "traditional faith" he lays hands on the life of the faithful, their raison d'être. *Heresy is at once blasphemy towards God and a curse for man.*[1]

In the previous section I have tried to explain the Orthodox understanding of salvation on its own terms, with as few references as possible to Protestant or Roman Catholic ideas about salvation. However, it is im-

[1] Archimandrite Vasileios, *Hymn of Entry* (Crestwood, NY: SVS Press, 1984), pp. 20-21.

possible to live in America at the beginning of the twenty-first century without being confronted with heterodox ideas about what it means to be saved. Indeed the popular understanding of the word "salvation" itself has been shaped by Evangelical Protestantism and the American history of revivalism. It is incumbent, therefore, on anyone who tries to explain the Orthodox doctrine of salvation to also explain why popularly held notions are incorrect

Most of the erroneous opinions that we shall discuss below are rooted in a misunderstanding of more fundamental elements of theology. In other words, heterodox ideas about salvation can be traced to heterodox ideas about God, Himself. Therefore, we need to say a few words about the importance of doctrine.

It is not uncommon in our day and age for people to dismiss doctrine as something that is either unimportant or even dangerous. What does it matter what you believe about God or how you worship Him (or Her or It?), so long as you love God and lead a good moral life? Is not a slavish devotion to doctrine the cause of religious strife? "Love unites; doctrine divides."

However popular these ideas may be, they are not only incorrect, they are spiritually dangerous. Orthodox Christianity cannot be compartmentalized. That is, one cannot separate doctrine from worship or ethics. We worship and live the way we do *because* we believe what we do about God. Similarly, what we believe about God is revealed and expressed by how we worship and live.

We must remember that the object of Orthodox Christianity is not to produce good, moral people. One does not need to be a Christian in order to live a moral, upstanding life. Rather, the goal is to become by grace what God is by nature. That is, our goal as Orthodox Christians is perfect God-likeness. To accomplish this, however, we must have a correct understanding of Who God is. Thus, correct doctrine is essential for man's salvation.

The Purpose of Doctrine

Before we examine how the Orthodox doctrine of God determines what we believe about salvation, we must first understand the purpose of doctrine. The Church does not make any claim to "explain" or "understand" God. On the contrary, we believe that this is impossible:

> For My thoughts are not your thoughts, neither are your ways My ways, saith the LORD. For as the heavens are higher than the earth, so are My ways higher than your ways, and My thoughts than your thoughts (Isa. 55:8-9).

In the Church, we often refer to doctrinal statements as "definitions." This is no accident. To define something literally means to put a fence around it, to separate the concept from ideas that do not belong to it. Thus, when the Church makes a definition about God, She is not trying to explain everything that can be said about God, but rather *excluding* ideas that are not appropriate to God. Orthodox theology, therefore, is often referred to as "apophatic" or negative theology.

For example, at the council of Chalcedon (A.D. 451), the Church said that in Christ the human and divine natures were united "without separation or division and without mixture or confusion." There is no way that we can rationally explain *how* God became man, so the Church defines how we ought *not* explain the mystery.

God is not an idea. He is not a mathematical concept or a geometric theorem. We cannot know Him simply by thinking. He is personal existence. To know Him we must enter into a personal relationship with Him. The Church's doctrinal statements, therefore, are designed to point us in the right direction and away from false paths.

Man Writ Large?

This emphasis on apophatic theology is as important in our own day as it was during the time of the great Church councils, for if there is one consistent trait of human nature, it is that we have the tendency to create images of God after our *own* image and likeness. Indeed, the nineteenth-century German philosopher Ludwig Feuerbach said that God was nothing more than a projection of the human mind—a human being idealized with superlative attributes. This notion was picked up by such thinkers as Karl Marx, Friedrich Nietzsche, Émile Durkheim, and Sigmund Freud.

Imputing human characteristics to God is called "anthropomorphizing." To be sure, in the Bible all sorts of things are said about God that fall into this category. For example, it is said that God walked in the Garden in the cool of the evening. There are references to His hands and ears and nostrils. However, when we read such things about God, we immediately realize that they are not meant to be taken literally. The Scripture says that God is spirit (cf. Jn. 4:24), so it is obvious that God does not have physical body parts. Thus, these anthropomorphisms are metaphorical.

Similarly, God does not have human emotions. He does not change. We say that God is *immutable*: He is *the same yesterday, today, and forever* (Heb. 13:8). This is very important, for the dominant ideas in Western culture about salvation are ultimately predicated on precisely this heretical notion: that God *does* change and that man can effect that change in God.

The Church's insistence on the "otherness" of God is itself rooted in the doctrine of creation *ex nihilo*. For the ancient Greeks, the world (*cosmos*) is eternal. For Plato, God is a craftsman (the *demiurge*) who makes things out of pre-existing matter. For Aristotle, God is the principle of movement, but He can in no way be considered the Creator (nor can He take part in the affairs of men, for He is "Thought thinking Itself" alone). For Israel and the Church, however, God is the Creator of all that is, and He created all that is from nothing: *Through faith we understand that the worlds were framed by the word of God, so that things which are seen were not made of things which do appear* (Heb. 11:3).

There is, therefore, an irreducible gulf between the uncreated Creator and the creation. Anything that we affirm about God must immediately be qualified, even the statement, "God exists." We cannot say that God exists in the same way that you or I or the world exists. Why? Because there was a time when you and I and even he world did *not* exist, and it is at least conceivable that we could *cease* to exist. Our existence has *non-existence* as its natural contrary, just as our being has *non-being* as its contrary. This is not the case with God, however. There was never a time when God was not, nor can there ever be a time when He will not be. God just *is: God said unto Moses, I AM THAT I AM* (Ex. 3:14). In other words, God has no natural contraries.[2]

For this reason, we must be very careful about what we say about God. This is why the Church has emphasized *apophatic* theology, emphasizing what God is *not* rather than trying to explain what He is.

[2] See St. Gregory Palamas: "Every nature is utterly remote and absolutely estranged from the divine nature. For if God is nature, other things are not nature, but if each of the other things is nature, He is not nature: just as He is not a being, if others are beings; and if He is a being, the others are not beings. If you accept this as true also for wisdom and goodness and generally all the things around God or said about God, then your theology will be correct and in accord with the saints." *The One Hundred and Fifty Chapters* 78, tr. by Robert Sinkewicz (Toronto: Pontifical Institute of Medieval Studies, 1988), p. 173.

Philosophical Distinctions

This does not mean, however, that we cannot say anything meaningful about God at all. Indeed St. Athanasius said that there would be no point in making man at all if God did not intend for us to know Him, our Maker. At every matins service the Church sings, *God is the Lord and hath appeared unto us.* When St. Paul went to Athens to preach, he addressed the philosophers of the city:

> *Then Paul stood in the midst of Mars' hill, and said, "Ye men of Athens, I perceive that in all things ye are too superstitious. For as I passed by, and beheld your devotions, I found an altar with this inscription, TO THE UNKNOWN GOD. Whom therefore ye ignorantly worship, Him declare I unto you. God that made the world and all things therein, seeing that He is Lord of heaven and earth, dwelleth not in temples made with hands; Neither is worshipped with men's hands, as though he needed any thing, seeing he giveth to all life, and breath, and all things; And hath made of one blood all nations of men for to dwell on all the face of the earth, and hath determined the times before appointed, and the bounds of their habitation; That they should seek the Lord, if haply they might feel after Him, and find Him, though He be not far from every one of us: For in Him we live, and move, and have our being; as certain also of your own poets have said, For we are also His offspring. Forasmuch then as we are the offspring of God, we ought not to think that the Godhead is like unto gold, or silver, or stone, graven by*

art and man's device. And the times of this igno-
rance God winked at; but now commandeth all men
every where to repent" (Acts 17:22-30).

The Christian God, therefore, is not an *Unknown God*,
but rather the God Who reveals Himself to those whose
hearts are pure: *Blessed are the pure in heart: for they shall*
see God (Mat. 5:8).

During the course of Christian history, when the
faithful were confronted by various heresies — false
ideas about God — the Church was forced to make certain philosophical distinctions in theology in order to
preserve right belief (literally, Orthodoxy). Once again,
these distinctions are not meant to be "explanations" of
God, for this is impossible, but rather signposts that
point us toward the living reality of God and away
from false impressions.

St. Gregory Palamas writes: "There are three reali-
ties in God, namely, substance, energy and a Trinity of
divine hypostases."[3] What he means by this is that we
make very important distinctions when talking about
God. We distinguish the nature from its energies or activities, and the Persons from the nature. As St. Gregory
himself points out, understanding these distinctions is
essential for understanding our salvation.

The first distinction was developed by the Church
in order to preserve the biblical doctrine of creation *ex*
nihilo. Origen, a third century theologian in Alexandria,
Egypt, stated that God was Creator *by nature.* Since
God's nature cannot change, He must have always been

---

[3] *The One Hundred and Fifty Chapters* 75, p. 171.

THE IMPORTANCE OF DOCTRINE

creating. This meant that the world is eternal. This is exactly what the pagan, Greek philosophers believed, but it is *not* what is revealed in the Bible. To combat this heretical "blurring" of the line between the Creator and creation, St. Athanasius drew a distinction between what God *is* and what He *does*. This distinction was further refined by St. Basil the Great and St. Gregory Palamas among others.

Had the Fathers not made this distinction, there would be no way to distinguish between the Son of God, Who is "begotten of the Father before all worlds," and the material creation, which God spoke into existence from nothing. St. Gregory writes:

> But if creating is not distinct from generation and procession, then creatures will in no way differ from the One begotten and the One sent forth. And if according to them this is the case, both the Son of God and the Holy Spirit will in no way differ from creatures, all creatures will be begotten and sent forth by God the Father, creation will become divine, and God will share His rank with creatures.[4]

The second distinction, between person and nature, was developed to help express as best we can the mysteries of the Holy Trinity and the Incarnation. The Church believes and confesses that the Word of God, one of the Holy Trinity, became man for our salvation. We also confess, however, that in becoming man He "remained what He was." That is, we believe that the

---

[4] *The One Hundred and Fifty Chapters* 96, p. 197.

Son of God became man, suffered, and died on the cross, and yet His divine nature underwent no change whatsoever. The only way that we can begin to make sense of this is to posit a real distinction between person and nature. The Second *Person* of the Trinity suffered in the flesh, but His divine *nature* did not suffer.

These same distinctions became important again in the sixth and seventh centuries during the so-called "monothelite" controversy. According to this heresy, our Lord Jesus Christ did not have a human will of His own. The Church reacted very strongly against this. If Christ did not have a human will, then how could He heal *our* will?

To solve this dilemma, the Fathers applied the person/nature/energies distinctions. Will is an energy or activity of nature. It is operated or exercised by the person. For example, we do not say that human nature chooses to do one thing or another, but that a particular *person* chooses to do something. In Christ, the human and the divine natures are united in one Person, the Son of God. Because will is an energy or activity of the nature, and because Christ possesses both a human as well as a divine nature, He therefore possesses a human will along with His divine will. However, because Christ is one Person and not two, He "exercises" His human will in complete conformity with the divine will. Thus, Jesus prayed in the Garden of Gethsemane: *not My will, but Thine, be done* (Luke 22:42).

The fact that the Fathers invoked these distinctions in respect to Christ and His human nature as well as in respect to God is very important. This means that we can also speak of humanity in terms of person, energy or activity, and nature. In other words, each human person shares a common human nature and common capacities, but each person will express his humanity and exercise his capacities in a way that is uniquely his own. Many of the modern misunderstandings about the nature of salvation are rooted in the failure to understand this basic element of Christian theology. We shall discuss these in the chapters that follow.

CHAPTER EIGHT

Reflection

1. What does what we believe about God have to do with our salvation?

2. What is the ultimate goal of Orthodox Christianity?

3. What is the purpose of a doctrinal definition?

4. Does the Church claim to know the nature of God?

5. What is "apophatic" theology mean?

6. What do we call it when we impute human attributes to God?

7. Are these statements to be understood literally or metaphorically? Why?

8. How is the Orthodox doctrine of creation related to what we can or cannot say about God?

9. What *can* we know about God?

10. What philosophical distinctions does the Church invoke in order to express a correct understanding of the Trinity and the Incarnation?

CHAPTER NINE

The Meaning of *Theosis*

Man outwardly seems to be merely a biological being, like the other living creatures, the animals. Of course, man is an animal, but, as St. Gregory the Theologian characteristically said, "Man is the only creature that stands apart from all creation, the only one that can become a god." ... It is, perhaps, very audacious even to say and think that our life's purpose is to become gods by Grace. However, the Holy Bible and the Fathers of the Church did not conceal this from us.[1]

The Orthodox doctrine of salvation is often misunderstood by Protestants and Roman Catholics alike. One of the primary stumbling blocks is the notion that salvation is ultimately a matter of *theosis*, or "deification." St. Athanasius wrote that God became man that man might become divine. This disturbs many people, who see in Orthodoxy a revival of the pagan confusion between man and God.

[1] Archimandrite George (Capsanis), *The Deification as the Purpose of Man's Life* (Mt. Athos: Holy Monastery of St. Gregory, 1997), pp. 12-13. The reference is to St. Gregory's "Homily on the Epiphany", PG 36, 324.13.

CHAPTER NINE

Because the words, "deification" and "divinization" are so easily misunderstood in our culture, I prefer to use the Greek word, *theosis*. Of course, *theosis* means deification, but by using a Greek word that most people are not familiar with, it gives one the opportunity of explaining the concept without starting, as it were, in a "conceptual hole." In other words, if you tell someone that the Orthodox Church teaches the doctrine of *theosis*, that person will ask what *theosis* is. If, on the other hand, you say that Orthodoxy teaches deification, the person will immediately *assume* certain things and may not stay around for a clarification.

There are two mistakes that people have historically made in reference to the understanding of salvation. On the one hand, some people *confuse* the human with the divine and conclude that men are naturally divine or a part of the divinity. This is what most people think of when they hear the word, "deification." There is, however, an opposite mistake, and that is to draw such a sharp distinction between divinity and humanity that there can never be a real union of God and man. In an effort to avoid the first mistake most modern Protestants have fallen headlong into the second.

The doctrine of *theosis* must be understood within the larger framework of Christian doctrine, especially the fundamental statements about God that we discussed in chapter eight. If we keep these signposts in sight, we will not be led astray. On the other hand, those who make the mistakes about salvation mentioned above, do so because they fail to take seriously these basic doctrines.

THE MEANING OF THEOSIS

By Grace, Not by Nature

According to Mormon teaching, the God of this world was once a man on another planet. He "earned" his godhood. All Mormons hope to achieve a similar state of deification (complete with their own, individual planets). Indeed there is a little verse that sums up the Mormon doctrine quite well:

As man now is, God once was.
As God now is, man may be.

Needless to say, this is *not* what the Orthodox Church means by *theosis*. The Mormon concept of God really does not merit much attention at all. It is, frankly, absurd. However, there is a more dangerous and more widespread theory of deification, and it is this version, popular among New Agers and devotees of "eastern mysticism," that many people confuse with Orthodoxy.

According to this view, man does not become "a God" as in Mormonism; man is believed to already be divine or a part of the divinity. The key here is "actualization." One is urged to realize and actualize one's divine nature. This approach tends to be *pantheistic*; that is, it asserts that everything is God.

The Orthodox understanding of *theosis*, on the other hand, proceeds from the affirmation that God is fundamentally different from everything else. The Orthodox can agree with the Protestant theologian Karl Barth, who said that God is "wholly other." This is where the doctrine of creation *ex nihilo* and the Orthodox emphasis on apophatic theology come into play.

The Orthodox understanding of *theosis* is also based on the Christological definition of the Council of Chalcedon. At that council, the Fathers decreed that Christ's human and divine natures were united "without mixture or confusion and without separation or division." In other words, what the Church says about the deification of human nature is exactly what She says about Christ's human nature.

Man is not naturally divine. He is a creature and will always remain a creature. Just as Christ's human nature did not become mixed or confused with His divine nature, so we, in the resurrection, will not become mixed or confused with God. In Christ the human and divine natures remain distinct, and they shall remain so for all of eternity.

Thus, there is an irreducible gulf between the nature of God and the nature of man. The fact that this gulf is irreducible, however, does not mean that it is *irreconcilable*. St. Paul affirms that *God was in Christ reconciling the world unto Himself* (2 Cor. 5:19). The definition of Chalcedon not only affirms that there is no confusion between Christ's divine and human natures, it also affirms that they are united without separation or division. Therefore, it is as incorrect to separate Christ's divine and human natures as it is to mix them together.

Theosis by Participation

St. Peter affirms that we shall be *partakers of the divine nature* (2 Peter 1:4). If, however, there is such a radical difference between God and man, how can this be? The answer is to be found in the distinctions between person, nature, and energy mentioned in chapter eight. St. Gregory Palamas explains:

Since it has been shown above that those deemed worthy of union with God so as to become one spirit with Him (even as the great Paul has said, *He who clings to the Lord is one spirit with Him* [1 Cor. 6:17]) are not united to God in substance, and since all theologians bear witness in their statements to the fact that God is imparticipable in substance and the hypostatic union happens to be predicated of the Word and God-man alone, it follows that those deemed worthy of union with God are united to God in energy and that the spirit whereby he who clings to God and is one with God is called and indeed the uncreated energy of the Spirit and not the substance of God...[2]

St. Gregory says that man's union of God cannot be according to substance because of the gulf between the divine and human natures. On the other hand, man cannot be said to participate in the Persons of the Trinity. What is left, therefore, is participation in God's energies:

Those who have pleased God and attained that for wich they came into being, namely divinization—for they say that it was for this purpose that God made us, in order to make us partak-

2 *The One Hundred and Fifty Chapters* 75, p. 171.

ers of His own divinity—these then are in God since they are divinized by Him and He is in them since it is He who divinizes them. Therefore, these too participate in the divine energy, though in another way, but not in the substance of God. And so the theologians maintain that "divinity" is a name for the divine energy.[3]

It is absolutely crucial at this point to understand that while the divine energies are differentiated from the divine nature and the Persons of the Trinity, they are nonetheless divine and uncreated. When we participate in the divine energies, we are participating in God Himself, not a created intermediary.

This is a major point of difference between the Orthodox and Roman Catholic understandings of theology.[4] According to the Roman Catholic teaching, there is no real distinction between God's essence and His energies; therefore, the grace of God is not God Himself, but a created effect. But how can a created effect deify man?

The issue of the essence and energies of God rarely, if ever, comes up in Protestant theology. Nevertheless, Protestants have inherited the assumption that grace is created and that man has no possibility of direct participation in God. What is left, therefore, is the idea of

---

[3] *The One Hundred and Fifty Chapters* 105, p. 201.
[4] According to Metropolitan Hierotheos Vlachos, it is the *primary* difference. Cf. *The Soul After Death*, Tr. by Esther Williams (Levadia, Greece: Birth of the Theotokos Monastery, 1996), p. 181.

salvation as moral improvement.[5] Archimandrite George writes:

> They refrain from speaking of deification in order to avoid Pantheism. What then, according to them, remains as the purpose of man's life? Simply a moral improvement. Since man cannot be deified by divine Grace, by the divine energies, what is his life's purpose? Simply to improve morally and maintain. But moral perfection is not enough for man. It does not suffice us simple to become better than before, to do moral deeds. Our ultimate goal is to unite with holy God. This is the purpose for the creation of the universe. This is the desired goal. This is our joy, our happiness, our fulfillment.[6]

What Archimandrite George is saying here is that the deep thirst within man is not for mere moral improvement. One need not be a Christian or believe in God at all in order to live a morally upstanding life. Man's thirst is for nothing less than union with God. This union cannot take place, however, unless God in some way gives Himself to man. God gives himself to man through His divine energies. In this way man is truly united with God, truly participates in His unending and superabundant life, and yet remains man. The

---

[5] Many conservative Protestants would disagree with this assessment, saying that salvation has nothing to do with moral improvement, but rather with how God views man. We shall discuss this notion of salvation in the next chapter.

[6] *The Deification as the Purpose of Man's Life*, p. 32.

union of God and man is accomplished and at the same time the utter transcendence of God is protected. Man is united to God "without mixture or confusion *and* without separation or division."

Reflection

1. What does the word *theosis* mean?

2. What are the two basic mistakes that people often make in regard to understanding salvation?

3. How is the Orthodox concept of *theosis* different from the Mormon doctrine of deification?

4. What is "Pantheism"? How does it differ from Orthodoxy?

5. What did the Fathers of the Council of Chalcedon say about the relationship between the divine and human natures in Christ?

6. Explain the statement that the gulf between God and man is irreducible but not irreconcilable.

7. Can man participate in God's innermost nature? Why or why not?

8. Why is the distinction between God's essence and energies important for understanding salvation?

9. What are the consequences of denying this distinction?

10. Is grace created or uncreated?

CHAPTER TEN

Satisfaction

Starting from such a concrete and existential concept of sin, the Orthodox tradition has refused to confine the whole of man's relationship with God within a juridical, legal framework; it has refused to see sin as the individual transgression of a given, impersonal code of behavior which simply produces psychological guilt. The God of the Church as known and proclaimed by Orthodox experience and tradition has never had anything to do with the God of the Roman juridical tradition, the God of Anselm and Abelard; He has never been thought of as a vengeful God who rules by fear, meting out punishments and torment for men.[1]

If you begin with the assumption that grace is created and not the uncreated energy of God, then God and man must remain forever external to each other. This has tremendous consequences for how we view salvation. Salvation cannot be defined as union with God, but only in terms of a moral or legal relationship

[1] Christos Yannaras, *The Freedom of Morality*, tr. by Elizabeth Briere (Crestwood, NY: SVS Press, 1984), p. 35.

between man and God. This is precisely what happened in Western Christianity.

Satisfaction

The Scriptures present salvation as a multi-faceted reality. Many different metaphors and images are used to express different aspects of the mystery.[2] In the Middle Ages however, one theologian sought to reduce this multifaceted reality to one fundamental idea that would express the very nature of salvation. The theologian was Anslem (A.D. 1033-1109), the Archbishop of Canterbury.[3] His view of salvation is known as "the satisfaction theory." This theory has dominated all thought on the subject in the Christian West from his day till the present.

In *Cur Deus Homo* (*Why God Became Man*), Anselm argued that by sinning, man had committed an offence against God. Remember that in medieval Western Europe, crimes were not committed against the state,

---

[2] I discuss this topic in more detail in *The Truth: What Every Roman Catholic Should Know about the Orthodox Church* (Salisbury, MA: Regina Orthodox Press, 1999, pp. 76-104.

[3] Anslem was French and came to England in the wake of the Norman Conquest. He played a pivotal role in the Norman program of supplanting the indigenous Anglo-Saxon Church with Norman clergy and practice. However, Anselm, like Thomas Becket who would follow him in the twelfth century, clashed with the crown over the rights of the church. He spent most of his time in exile.

but against the person of the monarch.[4] This offence against God demanded "satisfaction" of God's honor and justice:

> The importance of a crime is measured in terms of the one against whom the crime is committed. Therefore, a crime against God, sin, is infinite in its import. But, on the other hand, only a human being can offer satisfaction for human sin. This is obviously impossible, for human beings are finite, and cannot offer the infinite satisfaction required by the majesty of God. For this reason, there is need for a divine-human,

---

[4] Even today, in England, legal cases are brought by "the Crown" vs. the alleged offender. Compare this personalization of the state in the person of the monarch with the American practice of bringing charges as "the State" or "the People" vs. the alleged offender. Jaroslav Pelikan traces the word *satisfaction* to the medieval penitential system, which may itself have been based on Germanic law: "The ecclesiastical system of satisfaction, moreover, may have contained echoes of civil law as well, in which, according to the ancient Germanic requirement of *wergild*, one was obliged to make good for a crime in accordance with the standing of the injured party in society. Since in this case God was the injured party, only *wergild* paid by one who was both God and man would have been adequate." *Jesus Through the Centuries: His Place in the History of Culture* (New Haven: Yale University Press, 1985), pp. 108. See also Jonathan Edwards: "So that sin against God, being a violation of infinite obligations, must be a crime infinitely heinous, and so deserving of infinite punishment. Nothing is more agreeable to the common sense of mankind, than that sins committed against any one, must be proportionally heinous to the dignity of the being offended and abused." From "The Justice of God in the Damnation of Sinners."

God incarnate, who through his suffering and death offers satisfaction for the sins of all humankind.[5]

Now there is no reason to suppose that Anselm had anything but the best of intentions in promulgating this theory. Indeed, he was *trying* to be faithful to the definition of Chalcedon and the Orthodox affirmation that Christ is *both* God and man. In order to render satisfaction to God, Christ had to be man, because it was man that owed the debt to God. At the same time, He had to be God, because only a being equal to God would be *worthy* to render satisfaction to God. Intellectually, it is a very satisfying theory. But is it true?

Before we discuss the problems with this theory, we need to say a few words about its influence. Jaroslav Pelikan writes:

> More than any other treatise between Augustine and the Reformation on any other doctrine of the Christian faith, Anselm's essay has shaped the outlook not only of Roman Catholics, but of most Protestants, many of whom have paid him the ultimate compliment of not even recognizing that their version of the wisdom of the cross comes from him, but attributing it to the Bible itself.[6]

Justo González agrees:

[5] Justo L. González, *The Story of Christianity*, Vol. 1 (San Francisco: Harper and Row, 1984), p. 313.
[6] *Jesus Through the Centuries*, pp. 106-107.

This view of the work of Christ, which was by no means the generally accepted one in earlier centuries, soon gained such credence that most western Christians came to accept it as the only biblical one.[7]

Not everyone who followed Anselm agreed with the details of his theory. One could stress one or more aspects of the theory more than others. Some emphasized that it was the divine sense of justice that needed to be satisfied. Others focused on the slight to God's honor. Still others focused on the wrath of God that needed to be assuaged. Regardless of the points of emphasis, however, the basic outline of Anselm's doctrine was accepted by almost everyone.

Although the Protestant Reformers rejected much of Roman Catholic teaching, they too accepted the Anselmian concept of satisfaction. Indeed, the main point of contention between Roman Catholics and Protestants was not over whether or not God's justice, honor or wrath needed to be satisfied, but whether man could add anything to that satisfaction in penance.[8]

Let us jump forward a few centuries to our own day. The theory of satisfactionism lies behind the Gospel of salvation preached by Evangelical Protestants such as Billy Graham. Indeed there is a story told about

[7] *The Story of Christianity*, pp. 314-315.

[8] Jaroslav Pelikan, *The Christian Tradition*, Vol. 4, *Reformation of Church and Dogma (1300-1700)* (Chicago: University of Chicago Press, 1985), p. 324.

Billy Graham that illustrates how the concept is understood and expressed by modern Evangelicals.[9]

One day Billy Graham was late for a meeting and sped through a small town. The local police pulled him over and issued a ticket. Now the justice of the peace in the town was also the town barber. Mr. Graham was taken to the barbershop and presented to the barber/JOP. He informed Mr. Graham of the amount of the fine and then took that amount out of the shop cash register and paid the fine himself. This he did to illustrate the fact that Christ has paid humanity's "fine" owed to the justice of God.

Although this story may strike us as being simplistic, we should not be so quick to dismiss the power of such stories. The doctrine of satisfactionism has tremendous *psychological* attraction. There are very few people in the world who are not aware at least to some degree of their own shortcomings. Once a sense of psychological guilt is established, then the Good News is presented: Christ has *already* satisfied the Father's justice, wrath, and wounded honor. All man needs to do is "accept" what Christ has done. Man is then freed from his guilt.

It is possible for someone to walk into a revival meeting or evangelistic "crusade" and, within an hour, be overcome with a sense of guilt before a just God and a few minutes later be relieved of that guilt through a

[9] I have heard this story ascribed to Billy Graham, but I cannot vouch for the accuracy of the attribution. Whether Billy Graham is the source of the story or not, it is nonetheless a good illustration of the Evangelical understanding of satisfactionism.

cathartic act such as answering an "altar call." From hell-bound sinner to eternally secure saint in less than sixty minutes![10] *Psychologically* it is all very compelling. *Theologically*, however, it leads man away from the true God.

Dissatisfied

There are three (at least!) theological problems with the doctrine of satisfactionism. First, it is predicated upon the assumption that God has human characteristics. Second, it makes sin to be God's problem rather than man's. Third, it turns salvation into something wholly external to man, leaving him essentially *unchanged*.

In chapter eight we said that a correct understanding of salvation must be based on the fundamental doctrines about God. One of those doctrines is that God *does not change*.[11] Anger and pride are human emotions—and not the noblest ones at that! It is nothing

---

[10] Actually it does not even take sixty minutes. On the web site of the Bellevue Baptist Church of Memphis (Cordova), TN, there is a page entitled "Eternal Life." It begins with the question, "Did you know that the Bible tells how you can know for sure that you have eternal life and will go to be with God in Heaven?" It then explains the plan of salvation (according to Southern Baptists). At the end of the page the reader finds: "Welcome to God's family! If you have truly repented (forsaken, turned away) from your sins, placed your trust in Jesus Christ's sacrificial death, and received the gift of eternal life, you are now a child of God! Forever!" From sinner to saint in three minutes!

[11] Cf. James 1:17.

short of blasphemous to base an understanding of salvation on the idea that God gets angry or has a brittle ego. Anselm's God is not the God of the Church, but a medieval monarch projected into the heavens.

But what about all of those Bible verses that mention the wrath of God? To this I reply, what about all those verses that mention God's hands or ears? Why do we immediately recoil from thinking that God has physical body parts, yet have no trouble attributing human emotions to him?[12]

Let us consider anger for a moment. If we accept the notion that the sin of man angers God, then before man sinned, God was not angry. And, as the theory goes, after Christ's satisfaction of the divine anger, God is no longer angry. There is no way around it: God changes, and it is the action of man that causes the change.

Even if we throw out the notions of divine anger or wounded honor on the basis that they violate the most basic elements of Christian theology, what about the justice of God? God is just, and because He does not change, He cannot simply let man "off the hook." Justice must be satisfied.

Reread the last two sentences carefully: God *cannot* let man off the hook because of justice. According to this view, God Himself is subject to some sort of cosmic justice. Justice is, in a sense, greater than God.

---

[12] Mormons would argue that because we have no trouble attributing human emotions to God, we should have no trouble attributing a physical body to Him.

Even in medieval times theologians realized there was a problem with this. One solution was to invoke the sovereign will of God. Pelikan explains:

> For if, as Anselm's critics both ancient and modern have charged, he seemed to subject God to his own justice and law as though these were independent entities, the stress on the freedom of God now led to the principle: "The will of God is the norm and ground [*regula et origo*] of justice." Hence a human act was intrinsically good not in and of itself, but only by virtue of its having been defined as good by the free and sovereign will of God.... for God willed whatever he wanted to will, and both justice and mercy were names for the expression of that will as it was perceived.[13]

Unfortunately, this approach does not help matters much. Instead of making God subordinate to cosmic justice, it makes Him capricious. Could God have saved mankind some other way than by requiring the blood of His Son to be shed? Yes. He is God; He can do what He wants. Why did He not simply *forgive* man? He *chose* not to.[14] According to Jonathan Edwards, the only reason God has not *already* thrown all sinners into hell is

---

[13] *Reformation of Church and Dogma*, pp. 25-26.

[14] "Mankind could have perished, or a sinless man might have saved it, or each person might have been granted the grace to merit salvation individually — any of these, depending on what the will of God decreed." Pelikan, *Reformation of Church and Dogma*, p. 26.

because of His "mere arbitrary will, and uncovenanted, unobliged forbearance of an incensed God."[15]

Anselm, therefore, has succeeded in painting God into a corner. Either He changes, or He is subject to an external cosmic justice, or He is capricious. Such are the problems that arise when we attribute human characteristics to God. Hear again what God has to say on the subject:

> For My thoughts are not your thoughts, neither are your ways My ways, saith the LORD. For as the heavens are higher than the earth, so are My ways higher than your ways, and My thoughts than your thoughts (Isa. 55:8-9).

The second problem with satisfactionism is that it makes sin God's problem rather than man's. According to one version of the theory, the need for Christ to satisfy God's justice came about as a result of the tension between God's justice and His mercy. God *wants* to save man because He is merciful, but He *cannot* violate His own justice. Sin, therefore, is actually a problem for God. What is at issue here is not what sin actually *does* to humans, but what *effect* it has on God and His attitude toward man. Jonathan Edwards writes:

> The God that holds you over the pit of hell, much as one holds a spider, or some loathsome insect over the fire, abhors you, and is dreadfully provoked: his wrath towards you burns like fire; he looks upon you as worthy of noth-

---

[15] From "Sinners in the Hands of an Angry God."

ing else, but to be cast into the fire; he is of
purer eyes than to bear to have you in his sight;
you are ten thousand times more abominable in
his eyes, than the most hateful venomous serpent is in ours.[16]

The whole plan of salvation reduces to nothing
more than a fiction, an elaborate play whereby God can
declare man to be justified irregardless of man's actual
state. In the Christian East, the dominant metaphors for
understanding sin and salvation are sickness and
health. Translating the satisfaction theory into medical
categories demonstrates the absurdity of satisfactionism. It is analogous to saying that sickness affects the
doctor rather than the patient and that cure depends on
the doctor's attitude toward the patient rather than the
actual health of the patient.

This leads to the third problem with satisfactionism:
salvation remains external to man, and, therefore, man
remains fundamentally *unchanged*. To be sure, salvation
removes man's guilt, but what is guilt other than man's
moral standing before God? Yannaras writes,

But this justification of man purely through
faith in the expiatory power of Christ's death
on the cross does not mean that his sins are
blotted out, but merely that they are not
charged to him. Man remains in *essence* sinful...[17]

[16] From "Sinners in the Hands of an Angry God."
[17] *The Freedom of Morality*, p. 153, n12.

Throughout the entire process of salvation, God and man remain wholly *extrinsic* to one another. Man is in no sense changed or recreated, merely *declared* "not guilty." This is so because Satisfactionism presupposes the same underlying principle as Nestorianism: God and man cannot really be united on any level beyond that of moral obedience.

For Orthodoxy, however, the situation is quite the reverse. Fr. John Meyendorff notes:

> The whole problem is not a juridical and utilitarian one—what is sufficient, and what is not—but rather a question of the original human destiny, which is to be *with* God and *in* God. This original human destiny has been restored in Christ, the New Adam . . . What He is by nature, we become by grace.[18]

Orthodox Christianity, therefore, must reject the satisfaction theory of the atonement because it violates the most fundamental principles of Christian theology *and* because it leaves man fundamentally unchanged. For the Orthodox, to be saved is to be restored to true spiritual health. It is not God's attitude toward man that needs to be changed, but rather man's state.

---

[18]John Meyendorff, "The Significance of the Reformation in the History of Christendom" in *Catholicity and the Church* (New York: SVS Press, 1983), p. 73.

CHAPTER TEN

Satisfied Love

The idea of satisfactionism was so pervasive in the Christian West that it was inevitable that it would find its way into the Orthodox world. Indeed, Orthodox theologians often speak of a "Western Captivity" of Orthodox theology, when Orthodox textbooks and schools were strongly influenced by Western Christian ideas. However, while this influence was sometimes very strong, the self-understanding of the Orthodox Church as expressed in Her doctrine and liturgy was never significantly altered. In short, the Orthodox Church has never accepted the satisfaction theory as true, even though some individual theologians may have expressed the idea.

One theologian who seemingly comes very close to satisfactionism is St. Nicholas Cabasilas. His treatment of the atoning work of Christ is found in an excursus within his discussion of the Eucharist in his monumental, *The Life in Christ*. Written in the fourteenth century, his treatise evidences his acquaintance with the theology of Anselm of Canterbury.[19] Indeed, in the section under consideration he sounds positively *Anselmian*:

> The commission of sin involves injury to God Himself . . . Yet it is impossible for him to compensate for this insolence by any honour, particularly when he is in many ways indebted to

[19]Orthodox theologians of the day were well aware of the currents within Latin theological circles. St. Nicholas Cabasilas could be both harshly critical of Roman Catholicism and at the same time appreciative of various aspects of Latin theology and liturgy.

Him whom he has injured, and He who is injured is so far superior that the distance between them cannot even be measured. He, then, who seeks to cancel the indictment against himself must restore the honour to Him who has been insulted and repay more than he owes, partly by way of restitution, partly by adding compensation for the wrong which he as done . . . Wherefore, since we by our own means and of ourselves were unable to display righteousness, Christ Himself became for us "righteousness from God and consecration and redemption" . . . He alone, then, was able to render all the honour that is due to the Father and make satisfaction for that which had been taken away.[20]

Taken alone and completely out of context, these statements would indeed give patristic support for Satisfactionism. One should not, however, be too quick to "impute" the heresy of Satisfactionism to St. Nicholas. If one bothers to read the *entire* excursus, one discovers that while St. Nicholas uses the language of Satisfactionism, he in fact turns the idea on its head.

First of all, we should reiterate the fact that the section on the atonement is an excursus within a work on sacramental mysticism. The notion of soteriology as a separate "branch" of theology is a peculiar western aberration that stems from a failure to understand the Christian Faith as a seamless whole. St. Nicholas treats

[20]St. Nicholas Cabasilas *The Life in Christ*, pp. 117-118.

the subject within the overall framework of our participation in Christ's life. He does *not* view salvation as merely legalistic justification, but as true union with God in Christ:

> Union with Christ, then, belongs to those who have undergone all that the Saviour has undergone, and have experienced and become all that He has. Now He was united to blood and flesh pure from all sin. By nature He Himself is God from the very beginning, and that which He afterwards assumed, human nature, He has deified. Finally, he died for the sake of the flesh, and rose again.

> He who seeks to be united with Him must therefore share with Him in His flesh, partake of deification, and share in His death and resurrection. So we are baptized in order that we may die that death and rise again in that resurrection. We are chrismated in order that we may become partakers of the royal anointing of His deification. By feeding on the most sacred bread and drinking the most divine cup we share in the very Flesh and Blood which the Saviour assumed.[21]

Keeping this context in mind, let us now return to St. Nicholas' excursus on the atonement. Having established that the Father's honor has been offended by the

---

[21]Cabasilas, pp. 65-66.

sin of man, he goes on to explain how it is that the Son repays that debt of honor:

> The death which He died upon the cross to the Father's glory He brought in to outweigh the injury which we had committed; in addition, He most abundantly made amends for the debt of honour which we owed for our sins. By His life He paid all honour, both that which it befitted Him to pay and also that by which the Father ought to be honored.[22]

Christ honored the Father in His human life by fulfilling all the commandments of God, exemplifying "the heavenly philosophy on earth," and by performing many miracles to the glory of God the Father.

Christ's *sinless* life, however, does not exhaust the mystery of Christ's saving work. The very *fact* of the incarnation itself is a manifestation of God's glory and honor and reveals the true nature of God's honor:

> In addition to all these things, who does not know that by the very fact that He was among men and thus fully united with our flesh Christ most clearly and evidently showed forth the kindness and love for mankind of Him who sent Him, and thus rendered the glory which was the Father's due?[23]

---

[22]Cabasilas, p. 118.
[23]Cabasilas, pp. 118-119. The emphasis upon the whole economy of the Incarnation, not just the crucifixion, is common among the Fathers of the Church, especially St. Athanasius.

At this point, St. Nicholas begins to turn the idea of Satisfaction on its head. What is the honor due to God which man's sin has so grievously wounded? St. Nicholas answers succinctly: "For in what else could the honour of God consist than in being shown to be pre-eminently good?"[24] It is God's *goodness* against which man has transgressed. But this is not goodness conceived of as moral rectitude (precisely the mistake of those who wish to reduce Christianity to legalism and moralism); it is goodness defined as infinite love:

> It is obvious that in the Saviour we have come to know the utmost limit of God's love for man. By the things which He has done He alone taught men how God loves the world and how great is His concern for mankind.[25]

St. Nicholas now presents us with a paradox. God's honor and glory is His supreme goodness and love. What honor, then, could man possibly offer that would be commensurate with such love and goodness?

> This is the glory that was His due from of old; yet it was possible for no human being to offer it to Him. Therefore He says, "if I am a Father, where is my honour?" (Mal. 1:6). The only-begotten Son alone was able to fulfill all that is the Father's due.[26]

---

[24]Cabasilas, p. 119.
[25]Cabasilas, p. 119.
[26]Cabasilas, p. 119.

Here, we have moved beyond the concept of satisfaction for God's "wounded honor." Only the eternal, only-begotten Son of the Father, Who is the express image of the Father's person and glory, can render to the Father the glory due His eternal glory and honor. By becoming man and manifesting the love and goodness of God in human flesh, Christ *as man* renders the honor due to the Father. In this way, man's sin—his *failure* to love and reflect the goodness of God—is overcome by the love of God made flesh:

> If, then, the Father had no greater or better graces to give than those which He bestowed on human nature at the descent of His only-begotten Son, it is clear that man could have rendered no glory to God greater than that which the kindness and love that he has already received from Him already proclaim. For this reason the Saviour honours the Father through Himself in a manner befitting Himself and Him who has begotten Him.[27]

St. Nicholas' God is not the *angry* God who dangles sinners over hell like a spider over an open flame. Yes, man has sinned against God and offended His honor and glory. But God's honor and glory consists precisely in His infinite love and goodness. Man has sinned, not against some legal code, but against love, and only a love stronger than man's failure to love can heal the situation. The Song of Songs speaks of a *love as strong as death* (8:6). This is the love of God toward us! The cross

[27]Cabasilas, p. 119.

is the summit of God's love, not the emblem of His sadistic thirst for bloody retribution.

St. Nicholas Cabasilas was able to use the language of Satisfactionism not only because it was current in the time in which he wrote, but also because such language is in the Scriptures. However, forensic language is not the *only* language used to describe mankind's salvation. Indeed, the word "salvation" itself means to be made whole, to be "healed." The mistake made Anselm and his unfortunate followers was to isolate soteriology from the whole of Christian theology and then to reduce it to a mere legal transaction. By treating the atonement within the overall context of traditional, incarnational theology, St. Nicholas was able to utilize some of the favorite themes of the Latin tradition while at the same time keeping the necessary balance.

Reflection

1. Who is the originator of the "satisfaction theory" of the atonement?

2. According to the satisfaction theory, how is man saved?

3. How does the modern, Evangelical theory of salvation reflect Anselm's view.

4. What is the psychological attraction of this theory?

5. What does the satisfaction theory imply about the nature of God?

6. Why is this unacceptable?

7. In what way does satisfactionism make sin to be God's problem?

8. Does satisfactionism bring true healing to man?

9. How does satisfactionism differ from the Orthodox understanding of salvation?

10. How did St. Nicholas Cabasilas turn the idea of satisfactionism on its head?

CHAPTER ELEVEN

Faith vs. Works

Some without fulfilling the commandments think that they possess true faith. Others fulfil the commandments and then expect the kingdom as a reward due to them. Both are mistaken. A master is under no obligation to reward his slaves; on the other hand, those who do not serve him well are not given their freedom.[1]

There is probably no issue regarding man's salvation that has engendered more controversy than the relationship between faith and works. The problems started during biblical times, when people began misinterpreting the words of St. Paul. Some assumed that if one had "faith" then one did not need to lead a Christian life. To this misunderstanding St. James replied:

What doth it profit, my brethren, though a man say he hath faith, and have not works? Can faith save him? If a brother or sister be naked, and destitute of daily food, and one of you say unto them, "Depart in peace, be ye warmed and filled;" notwithstanding ye

---

[1] St. Mark the Ascetic, "On Those who Think that They are Made Righteous by Works: Two Hundred and Twenty-Six Texts" 18-19 in the *Philokalia*, Vol. 1, p. 126.

give them not those things which are needful to the body; what doth it profit? Even so faith, if it hath not works, is dead, being alone. Yea, a man may say, "Thou hast faith, and I have works: show me thy faith without thy works, and I will show thee my faith by my works." Thou believest that there is one God; thou doest well: the devils also believe, and tremble. But wilt thou know, O vain man, that faith without works is dead (James 2:14-20)?

It is important to note here that St. James is not disagreeing with St. Paul, as Luther and many other Protestants have mistakenly thought, but rather he is disagreeing with a misinterpretation of St. Paul's statement, *Therefore we conclude that a man is justified by faith without the deeds of the law* (Rom. 3:28).[2] Clearly St. Paul is referring to "works of the law," meaning the Jewish law. His point is that man cannot make himself righteous simply by following the law. He does *not* mean — and this is what St. James wanted to show — that works play no part in man's salvation.

Protestantism vs. Roman Catholicism

Protestants often frame the issue in terms of a stark — and false — dichotomy: man is saved *either* by faith alone *or* by works. If man is saved by works, then what Christ accomplished on the cross was not sufficient for salvation. This is impossible, for Christ accomplished what man could not. He made satisfaction to

---

[2] Luther referred to the Epistle of James as a "straw epistle" and moved it to the back of his Bible.

God for man's sin. If man could work his way into heaven, then there would have been no need for Christ's sacrifice. Therefore, salvation comes about solely through faith in Christ and His sacrifice, not at all through works.

Such an argument contains so many leaps in logic it is hard to know where to begin. For one thing, because man is not justified by performing the works of the law (St. Paul), it does not necessarily follow that man is saved by faith *alone*. This was St. James' point. Furthermore, the argument that human works *detract* from what Christ has done *presupposes* that salvation is a state extrinsic to man's actual spiritual condition. In other words, it presupposes the theory of salvation as satisfaction.

If we begin by assuming that sin is an affront to God's honor that demands an infinite satisfaction, and if we further assume that only the infinite Son of God could make that infinite satisfaction on behalf of man, then all that remains is to determine *how* that satisfaction is applied to individual people. Everyone at the time of the Reformation, both Roman Catholic and Protestant, insisted on the necessity of faith in Christ. The question was, "Is anything further required?"

According to Roman Catholic theology, the sin of man incurs both an eternal and a temporal punishment. Christ has made satisfaction for the eternal punishment, but not the temporal. Therefore, the sacrament of penance is necessary in order to make satisfaction for the temporal punishment due to sin. If a Christian dies without making such satisfaction, he or she goes to purgatory, where satisfaction is made through suffering. After this purging, the soul is allowed into heaven. The system of "indulgences" developed as a way to reduce one's time in purgatory.

The Protestant reaction to this was understandable. How could the sacrifice of Christ not be sufficient to pay the *whole* debt of sin? We saw in the last chapter that the difference between Roman Catholics and the major Reformers in regard to satisfaction was whether the system of penances could *add* anything to Christ's satisfaction. The Protestant answer was "no." The Orthodox *would* agree with this, *if only* we accepted the framework of salvation as satisfaction.

Calvinism vs. Arminianism

The Reformers latched onto the concept of justification by *faith alone* as the very cornerstone of the Gospel. However, another problem immediately presented itself. Is faith itself not a work? Is it not something that the Christian *does*? Questions like these led to what is known as the Arminian controversy.

Jacob Arminius was a Dutch Calvinist who came to the conclusion that the prevailing Calvinist doctrine of predestination was incorrect. Classical Calvinism teaches that before the world was formed, God had predestined some to be vessels of election and some to be vessels of wrath, and this *without* any reference to His foreknowledge. In other words, God's election of the saved is unconditional; it is in no way dependent upon anything the elect might do or not do. Arminius, on the other hand, said that God's election was conditional upon man's faith. For the Calvinists, God does *everything*. For Arminians, man, in however limited a way, *cooperates* with God in faith.

The result of this controversy was the definition of Calvinism put forth by the Synod of Dort. This is the famous five-point summary of Calvinism that goes by the acronym of TULIP:

T = Total Depravity. Because of the sin of Adam, all men are totally depraved and incapable of *any* good work.

U = Unconditional Election. God's election of the saved is in no way dependent on anything they may do.

L = Limited Atonement. Christ's saving work is limited to the Elect. Christ did not die for those predestined for hell.

I = Irresistible Grace. God's grace and election cannot be resisted by man. Man cannot say, "No," to God.

P = Perseverance of the Saints. Those elected by God to be saved will persevere to the end and shall not fall away from grace.

While it is certainly true that TULIP did not originate with Calvin himself, it is, nonetheless, a logical deduction from his theology. From a Calvinist viewpoint, therefore, faith must be conceived of as merely a passive state in which God acts upon man and to which man can contribute nothing.

Thus, we not only have Protestants debating Roman Catholics on the subject of the relationship between faith and works, we have Calvinists debating Arminians on whether or not faith is an active work of man or merely a passive state wrought by God. From the Synod of Dort until today, the vast majority of Evangelical Protestants have found themselves caught in the middle of this tug of war.

American Evangelicalism has historically been Calvinistic—at least on the surface. However, American Calvinists have rarely been *orthodox* Calvinists. Indeed, by the time Calvinism hit the shores of England and Scotland and was enshrined in the Westminster Confession, it had undergone subtle, but significant changes. In America, revivalism, with its emphasis on conversion, exemplified a strange mixture of both Calvinism and Arminianism. This mixture has characterized most of American Evangelicalism to this day.[3]

According to most modern Evangelicals, man is saved by faith alone, but faith is encapsulated in some sort of conversion experience. Man makes a "decision" whether or not to place his faith in Christ.[4] This is much closer to Arminianism than it is to classical Calvinism.

---

[3] Cf. Philip Lee's critique of contemporary Protestantism, *Against the Protestant Gnostics*. Oxford: Oxford University Press, 1987.

[4] Indeed, the language of "decision" is central to modern Evangelicalism. The word itself is often employed in the title of

CHAPTER ELEVEN

Lordship Salvation vs. Free Grace

However, even within Evangelicalism, there is a further dispute. During the last couple of decades there has been a debate among Evangelical Protestants over something called "Lordship Salvation." According to this view, saving faith in Christ implies a life of obedience to Christ.[5] On the other side of the fence are those who believe that faith is a simple act of belief or trust and no more. The proponents of Lordship Salvation accuse the advocates of "Free Grace" of preaching "Easy Believeism" and a Gospel of "Cheap Grace."[6] The proponents of Free Grace, on the other hand, accuse the

radio and television shows. The magazine of the Billy Graham Evangelistic Association is called *Decision*.

[5] According to one proponent, "Lordship Salvation" affirms that "true saving faith includes in it a submission to the Lordship of Christ." See Richard P. Belcher, *A Layman's Guide to the Lordship Controversy* (Southbridge, MA: Crowne Publications, 1990), p. 92.

[6] "Easy Believeism" is a common epithet. The phrase, "Cheap Grace" comes from Dietrich Bonhoeffer. See his *The Cost of Discipleship* (New York: Macmillan, 1963), esp. pp. 45ff. "Cheap grace means the justification of sin without the justification of the sinner. Grace alone does everything, they say, and so everything can remain as it was before.... Cheap grace is the preaching of forgiveness without requiring repentance, baptism without church discipline, Communion without confession, absolution without personal confession. Cheap grace is grace without discipleship, grace without the cross, grace without Jesus Christ, living and incarnate" (pp. 46-47). Although there are numerous problems with Bonhoeffer's theology from an Orthodox perspective, there is nevertheless much that an Orthodox Christian can agree with in his critique of "cheap grace."

Lordship Salvation advocates of *adding* requirements to the Gospel.

What is fascinating about this whole debate is that it does not break down along the lines that one might expect. At first glance, one would expect Arminians to champion Lordship Salvation and Calvinists to champion Free Grace. However, almost the exact opposite is true. The chief proponents of Lordship Salvation are a who's who of contemporary Reformed theologians, including John Stott, J. I. Packer, and John MacArthur.[7] On the other hand many of the most vociferous opponents of Lordship Salvation are Arminians. The Dallas Theological Seminary, for example, has never been known as a center of Calvinistic thought, and some of the most vocal criticism of Lordship Salvation has come out of Dallas.[8]

---

[7] Keep in mind that most contemporary Calvinists are not orthodox Calvinists.

[8] Cf. the Doctrinal Statement of the Dallas Theological Seminary: "We believe that when an unregenerate person exercises that faith in Christ which is illustrated and described as such in the New Testament, he passes immediately out of spiritual death into spiritual life, and from the old creation into the new; being justified from all things, accepted before the Father according as Christ His Son is accepted, loved as Christ is loved, having his place and portion as linked to Him and one with Him forever. Though the saved one may have occasion to grow in the realization of his blessings and to know a fuller measure of divine power through the yielding of his life more fully to God, he is, as soon as he is saved, in possession of every spiritual blessing and absolutely complete in Christ, and is therefore in no way required by God to seek a so-called "second blessing," or a "second work of grace" (John 5:24; 17:23;

CHAPTER ELEVEN

A Different Framework

I bring up this long history of debates to illustrate the fact that the question is not as simple as many would have it. Even those who believe that man is saved by faith alone disagree about what faith is.

Furthermore, I want to underscore the fact that *all* of these debates presuppose the same framework: sin is conceived as a legal transaction that affronts God's honor and piques His wrath. It is, therefore, God's honor and justice that must be satisfied and God's anger that must be assuaged. Virtually nothing is said about man *except* his standing before God.

The Orthodox understanding of salvation, on the other hand, proceeds from very different premises.[9] As we saw in the last chapter, the idea that man's actions can cause a change in God—can make Him angry or offend Him—is nothing short of blasphemy.[10] God does

Acts 13:39; Rom. 5:1; 1 Cor. 3:21-23; Eph. 1:3; Col. 2:10; 1 John 4:17; 5:11-12)."

[9] My approach here is not to get into a verse-by-verse discussion of the faith vs. works controversy, but rather to underscore the different frameworks in which the Western and Orthodox conceptions of salvation were developed. For those wanting a detailed critique of the Protestant doctrine of *sola fide*, see Robert A. Sungenis, *Not by Faith Alone: The Biblical Evidence for the Catholic Doctrine of Justification* (Santa Barbara, CA: Queenship Publishing, Co., 1997. Sungenis is a Catholic apologist and therefore approaches the topic from within the same Western framework as do Protestants.

[10] The Calvinist solution to this problem is to lay everything at the feet of God's sovereign will. Man does nothing to invoke either God's wrath or His mercy. God has predestined *all* things, including the fall of man. This idea, known as *supralapsarianism*, is denied by many modern Calvinists, who do not want to face up to the real

not change. Furthermore, God does not undergo an internal struggle between His justice and His mercy. St. Isaac the Syrian said that we are *not* to call God just. He is not just; He is good and merciful and always acts with love and mercy toward His creatures.[11] For the Orthodox, sin is not a crime against the divine justice, but a sickness that destroys *man*. Christ came not to heal God's wounded honor but to heal *man* of his sickness. Because of sin, man had become enslaved to death and corruption. God is life, and man had cut himself off from the only source of life and happiness. Christ came to restore man to life.

Person and Nature

In Chapter nine we saw the importance of the fundamental doctrines of Christology in understanding the doctrine of salvation. In this chapter I want to underscore the importance of the distinction between person and nature. Understanding this distinction will help to

implications of Calvinism. "Hyper-Calvinism," however, is nothing but *real* Calvinism. Calvin did teach that God had foreordained all things, and *supralapsarianism* is the *only* rational outcome of Calvin's principles. Cf. *Institutes* 2.23.7.

[11] "Mercy and just judgment in one soul is like a man worshipping God and idols in the same house. Mercy is the opposite of just judgment.... As grass and fire cannot stay together in the same house, so neither can just judgment and mercy remain in one soul. As a grain o sand cannot compare in weight with much gold, so neither can the need for God's just judgment compare with His mercy." *Mystic Treatises* 58, quoted in Yannaras, *The Freedom of Morality*, p. 60 n6.

explain why the faith vs. works argument is simply not an issue for the Orthodox.

When we say that there is a distinction between person and nature, we mean that the person is not exhausted by or reducible to his nature. In Christology, we say that the *Person* of Christ suffered and died on the cross in the flesh, yet His divine nature remained unchanged. The heretic Nestorius, however, could not understand this. He argued that the Son of God could not be the subject of the crucifixion, because this would mean that His divine nature suffered. The man Jesus, who was somehow conjoined to the Word, was the subject of the crucifixion. In other words, for Nestorius, the person is nothing more than an individual instance of nature and no more.

For the Orthodox, it is the person that "possesses" the nature, that makes it be. In one sense, you are your nature; that is you are a human being because you possess human nature. Yet, you express that nature, which is common to all of us, in a way that is uniquely your own. There are billions of people on earth, but only one you. When we talk about salvation, therefore, we must talk not only about the restoration of human nature, but also about the restoration of the human *person*.

Because of the fall of Adam and Eve, human *nature* has become corrupted and enslaved to death. Man has not inherited the *guilt* for Adam's sin, but rather the *consequences* of that sin. These pertain to our nature. Furthermore, we have not only inherited a nature that is mortal, but one in which our natural faculties (energies) do not function properly. Our desires are oriented toward sensible things rather than toward spiritual, and our will is prone to choose the evil over the good. We as persons are, therefore, enslaved to a nature that is corruptible and oriented away from God. When Christ took human flesh from the pure Virgin and became man, He began the process of healing human nature. His human will was united to His divine will, and in an act of perfect obedience to the Father, He accepted to undergo death on the cross. Through His obedience He healed the human will, and through His death and resurrection He destroyed the power of death that held man captive, restoring human nature to true life.

This is the *objective* dimension of salvation. Christ *has* definitively saved human nature and bestowed upon it His own glory and immortality. However, there is a personal or *subjective* dimension of salvation. Even though all people will rise from the dead on the Last Day, not all people will experience the resurrection as something blessed.[12]

Perhaps an analogy will be helpful here. Imagine someone who is physically in the peak of health, but who is also jealous, petty, greedy and in general thoroughly egocentric. Would such a person be happy? In the resurrection, we will know health and natural well being as we have never known it before. There will be no sickness or death of any kind. And yet, there will be those who will not be happy, because their unhappiness is rooted not in their nature, but in their souls.

---

[12] Cf. Chapter five, above.

If salvation were a matter of God's attitude toward man rather than man's free participation in the life of God, then heaven would be filled with men and women who have been declared "not guilty" by God, yet whose souls are still corrupted with sin. Sin is not God's problem, but man's. Christ has done *everything* to restore human nature and open the gates of the kingdom for man, but whether we enter and enjoy that kingdom is up to us.

According to the Fathers, God will never overrule or destroy man's free will. God is love and He created man to live in an eternal communion of love with Him. However, love cannot be compelled. It must be free. Therefore, if man is to be healed of his spiritual sickness—his pride and egoism—then he must *cooperate* with God. St. Diadochos writes:

> All men are made in God's image; but to be in His likeness is granted only to those who through great love have brought their own freedom in subjection to God.... Free will is the power of a deiform soul to direct itself by deliberate choice towards whatever it decides.[13]

Here, St. Diadochos equates the image of God with man's nature, and the likeness of God with man's personal action. Christ has restored the image of God in man, but whether we attain to the likeness of God is up to each one of us. In other words, God can make us immortal, but He cannot make us good and loving.

[13] "On Spiritual Knowledge and Discrimination" 4-5 in the *Philokalia*, Vol. 1, pp. 253-254.

The Orthodox insistence on human cooperation with God (*synergeia*) takes nothing away from the work of Christ. Christ truly did do what man could not: He conquered the power of sin and death and restored all mankind to the image of God. Furthermore, it is only *in Christ*, that is, only in union with His Body, that man's person or soul is healed. As St. Paul told the Athenians, *For in him we live, and move, and have our being* (Acts 17:28).

Furthermore, the Orthodox doctrine of *synergy* does not mean that man "earns" his salvation on his own "merit." The whole concept of merit is foreign to Orthodoxy. Heaven is not a cosmic playground, and hell is not a cosmic torture chamber. When Christ returns in glory He will be *all in all*, and we shall experience His presence either as light and life and love or as judgment and condemnation. The difference will not be in Christ's attitude toward us—for He loves all without distinction or qualification—but rather in our *ability* to relate to Him. This is the *subjective* dimension of salvation; this is the realm of faith *and* works.

Reflection

1. How did the first controversy over the relationship between faith and works arise?

2. Was St. James disagreeing with St. Paul?

3. What statements about God does the Western debate about faith and works presuppose?

4. How is this debate related to the Western doctrine of satisfactionism?

5. Roman Catholics and Protestants agree on the need for faith in Christ; about what do they disagree?

6. Calvinists and Arminians agree that man is saved by faith and not works; about what do they disagree?

7. What is the difference between "Lordship Salvation" and "Free Grace"?

8. How is the Orthodox framework for viewing these issues different from that of Protestants or Roman Catholics?

9. How does the distinction between person and nature help us to understand this issue?

10. Can man be saved against his own will?

CHAPTER TWELVE

Once Saved,
Always Saved?

*Never believe in your own power and strength
to resist temptation of any kind, great or small.
Think, on the contrary: I am sure to fall as soon
as it comes upon me. Self-confidence is a dangerous confederate. The less strength you credit
yourself with, the more surely you stand. Ac-
knowledge that you are weak, completely unable to resist the slightest beckoning of the
devil. Then to your astonishment you will find
that he has no power over you. For if you have
made the Lord your refuge you will soon be
able to ensure that no evil shall befall you (cf.
Psa. 91). The only evil that can befall a Christian is sin.*[1]

The differences between Orthodox Christianity and
the Western confessions are not matters of mere ab-
stract theology; they extend to the most basic aspects of
personal piety as well. This clash of differing pieties is
clearly evident when an Orthodox Christian and an
Evangelical Christian discuss salvation. An Evangelical

[1] Tito Colliander, *Way of the Ascetics* (Crestwood, NY: SVS
Press, 1994), p. 53.

Christian feels secure in the knowledge that he or she is saved and expects anyone else who is really a Christian to feel equally secure. A pious Orthodox Christian, on the other hand, is normally reticent to make a declaration that he or she is definitely "saved." The Evangelical takes this as a sign that the Orthodox person does not really "know Jesus."

For the majority of Evangelical Protestants, it is possible for someone to know definitively that he or she is saved and rest secure in the knowledge that salvation can never be lost. These are the doctrines of "assurance" and "eternal security."[2] The Orthodox Christian can accept neither of these doctrines. In this chapter I shall explain why.

Blessed Assurance

There is no more self evident truth to Evangelicals than that one can be saved and know it:

> *These things have I written unto you that believe on the name of the Son of God; that ye may know that ye have eternal life, and that ye may believe on the name of the Son of God* (1 Jn. 5:13).

How can Orthodox Christians deny what is stated so plainly in the Scripture? The problem is that Orthodox and Evangelicals do not use the word "saved" in the same sense. In other words, we are talking about two very different things.

---

[2] Not all Evangelicals believe both. Strict Arminians, such as Methodists, Free Will Baptists, and Campbellites do not believe in eternal security.

The Evangelical understanding is rooted in the framework we have discussed in previous chapters. It presupposes the satisfaction theory of the atonement. It presupposes that the difference between the saved and the damned is the attitude of God toward them, not any inherent quality of their own. And, it presupposes that man's state — guilty or justified — can be changed in an instant.

To be "saved" means to be declared "not guilty" by God. It means that when God looks at us, He sees Christ's righteousness instead of our sinfulness. Through His substitutionary atonement on the cross, Christ has satisfied the Father's justice and honor and assuaged His wrath. Because the saved person stands before God "justified," that is cleared of all charges of sin against him, he can enter heaven and enjoy the blessed life that God has prepared for His elect.

On the other hand, those who reject Christ — that is, those who fail to deliberately "accept" Christ as their personal Lord and Savior — remain in their sin. When God looks at them, He sees not the righteousness of His Son, but the true, sinful state of the sinner. Sinners are cast into hell, which is the deserved punishment for all those who violate God's laws.

Within *this* framework, the doctrine of assurance makes perfect sense. If one has "accepted Christ" — placed his trust in Christ's atoning work — then one can be confident that God will keep His promise: *whosoever shall call on the name of the Lord shall be saved* (Acts 2:21). I have accepted Christ; therefore, I *am saved*. Nothing could be simpler.

CHAPTER TWELVE

For the Orthodox Christian, on the other hand, salvation is not a matter of how God views man. God always looks upon man with love, regardless of man's actions: *for He maketh His sun to rise on the evil and on the good, and sendeth rain on the just and on the unjust* (Mat. 5:45).[3] It is man's ability to relate to God, not God's ability to relate to man that is at issue.

We have already seen that Christ has definitively saved human nature. We have also seen, however, that there is a subjective or personal dimension to salvation. When, therefore, we talk about salvation, we mean a state of God-likeness through which we attain true union with God.

Because salvation ultimately refers to the actual spiritual state of the Christian, Orthodox Christians are rightly reticent to make pronouncements about their own salvation. To do so is to presume upon the judgment of God. When an Evangelical says that he is saved, he is not commenting upon the state of his own soul, but upon the fact that God no longer sees him as a sinner. On the other hand, for an Orthodox Christian to say that he is saved, would imply that he has himself attained a high level of righteousness before God.

The essence of the fall of man is pride. The core of man's spiritual sickness is his own egotism. In order for man to be healed, therefore, he must become humble;

[3] The context of this verse is extremely important. Here Christ is exhorting His followers to love their enemies. Anyone can love his friends, but it is a mark of God-likeness to love one's enemies. According to the satisfaction theory, however, God *hates* His enemies.

he must embrace the spiritual poverty of which the Lord spoke: *Blessed are the poor in spirit, for theirs is the kingdom of heaven.... Blessed are the pure in heart, for they shall see God* (Mat. 5:3, 8). The kingdom of heaven and the vision of God are not promised to those who have been "declared not guilty," but to those who are actually humble and pure of heart.

It is for this reason that the pious Orthodox Christian refrains from trying to evaluate his own spiritual life. It is a spiritual paradox that the closer one comes to God, the more *unworthy* one feels. Similarly, the further away one is from God, the more confident and self-assured (prideful) one feels. The greatest saints of the Church trusted in the grace of God, but never presumed that they were themselves holy. This story from the Desert Fathers is illustrative:

> It was said of Abba Sisoes that when he was at the point of death, while the Fathers were sitting beside him, his face shown like the sun. He said to them, "Look, Abba Anthony[4] is coming." A little later he said, "Look, the choir of prophets is coming." Again his countenance shone with brightness and he said, "Look, the choir of apostles is coming." His countenance increased in brightness and lo, he spoke with someone. Then the old men asked him, "With whom are you speaking, Father?" He said, "Look, the angels are coming to fetch me, and I am begging them to let me do a little penance." They said to him, "You have no need to do penance, Father." But

[4] St. Anthony the Great. He is often referred to as the father of monasticism, but he was not the first monk.

the old man said to them, "Truly, I do not think I have even made a beginning yet." Now they all knew that he was perfect. Once more his countenance suddenly became like the sun and they were all filled with fear. He said to them, "Look, the Lord is coming and He's saying, 'Bring me the vessel from the desert.'" Then there was as a flash of lightening and all the house was filled with a sweet odour.[5]

Here is a man that is so holy that his body literally shown with divine light, yet in his deep humility he begs for more time to repent. This is not a lack of trust in God, but a state of true humility and purity of heart. The saint says with Isaiah the Prophet: *Woe is me! For I am undone; because I am a man of unclean lips, and I dwell in the midst of a people of unclean lips: for mine eyes have seen the King, the LORD of hosts* (Isa. 6:5).

According to St. Isaac the Syrian, humility is to see oneself as lower than all of creation. A man who is truly humble will never judge anyone[6], will never take offence. If an evil befalls him, he will accept it as his due because of his sinfulness. If good should befall him, he will accept it as an undeserved gift of grace. To the humble man, all is grace and light; he shall inherit the kingdom of God.

Archimandrite George explains the importance of humility:

[5] Benedicta Ward, tr. *The Sayings of the Desert Fathers* (London: Cistercian Publications, 1975), pp. 214-215.
[6] Cf. Mat. 7:1.

The one who begins the journey to deification must have ceaseless humility in order to keep himself continually on this journey. For, if he accepts the thought that he is doing well and advancing on his own, then pride overtakes him. He loses whatever he had gained and needs to start anew, to be humble, to see his weakness, his human illness and not to rely on himself. He must rely on God's Grace in order to be kept continually on the journey to deification.

Do you see why humility is so important? The moment we think we have "arrived" is the moment pride sets in, and it is pride that separates us from God. Archimandrite George continues:

That is why, in the lives of our saints, we are impressed by their great humbleness. Although they were very close to God, shone in the light of God, worked miracles, gave forth myrrh, yet at the same time they held themselves in low esteem, believed they were far from God, that they were the worst of men. This very humility made them gods by Grace.[7]

Eternal Security or Infernal Delusion?

This brings us to the topic of eternal security. According to Archimandrite George and indeed all of the Church's spiritual writers, a man must be humble in

[7] *The Deification as the Purpose of Man's Life*, p. 38.

order to *stay on* the right path and attain that for which he seeks. In other words, success in the spiritual life is not guaranteed.

For Evangelical Protestants, on the other hand, few doctrines are as cherished as that of the eternal security of the believer.[8] Those who doubt this doctrine quickly run afoul of popular sentiment. Not only can you *know* that you are saved, you can know that you *cannot* fall away.

This doctrine is without doubt rooted in Calvinism, yet its real force is not doctrinal but psychological. Let us look briefly at each of these aspects.

Eternal security is a popularization of Calvinist doctrine of perseverance (the "P" in TULIP). According to the original version, those whom God has elected for salvation before the world began, shall persevere until the end and shall in no way fall from grace.

The doctrine of perseverance is, in fact, a necessary logical deduction from the other tenets of Calvinism. Since the elect have been chosen by God without any reference to their actions—there is absolutely nothing you or I can do to influence God's choice—and since God's grace is irresistible—you cannot refuse it even if you wanted to—then it make sense that there is nothing that you can do to lose your salvation. Perseverance has nothing to do with any "staying power" within the Christian, but solely with the power of God's will, which cannot be thwarted.

---

[8] For a list of denominations that do *not* subscribe to this doctrine, see note two above.

The interesting thing about this is that the doctrine of eternal security—the popularized concept of perseverance—is held by many that are not Calvinists. In fact, I would estimate that numerically, the *majority* of people who hold to this doctrine are not Calvinists. Take the Southern Baptist Convention, for example. This is the largest Protestant denomination in the United States. The *vast majority* of Southern Baptists hold to an Arminian theology of conversion, yet eternal security is one of the most sacrosanct of doctrines.[9]

The problem here is that what makes sense within a Calvinistic system does not make sense within an Arminian system. Arminians believe that man has the power to accept or to reject Christ, and that this determines his eternal destiny. Calvinists, on the other hand, deny that man has such power. It is because man has *no say* in his own salvation, that he cannot lose it. Arminians put man's destiny back in his own hands. How then can they claim that it cannot be lost?[10] Those who hold an Arminian theology of conversion and a Calvinist doctrine of perseverance are put in the odd position of saying that man has free will *until* he gets "saved," but is no longer capable of doing anything that will affect his salvation afterwards.

---

[9] In the early 1980's Dale Moody, a professor at the Southern Baptist Theological Seminary in Louisville, KY was forced into early retirement because he published a book in which he argued that it is possible for man to lose his salvation.

[10] Strict Arminians, of course, do teach that man can apostasize.

Being a three or four point Calvinist is rather like being three-fourths pregnant. From an Orthodox perspective, Calvinism is not only wrong, but also blasphemous. It is, however, internally consistent, and therein lies its charm for many people. One cannot simply pull out the perseverance of the saints and insert it into another theological system and expect it to make any sense.[11]

The vast majority of Evangelical Protestants, however, are not terribly concerned about whether their theology is internally consistent. The doctrine of eternal security — or "once saved, always saved" as it is sometimes known — has a tremendous psychological attraction for Christians. Consider this argument from a message by Adrian Rogers, a former president of the Southern Baptist Convention:

> Can you imagine the emotional state of a child who does not know from day to day whether or not he is a member of the family? Today, since he was a good boy, he is considered a member. But tomorrow, if he misbehaves, he may no longer be a member. Today he is loved by his father. Tomorrow he may not be. This child would be a neurotic mess! You are a part of your family, regardless of your behavior. So it is in the family of God, too. If you belong to

[11] This strange mixture of Arminianism and Calvinism was not the result of conscious experimentation, but rather the result of a slow transmutation of Calvinism in America due to the influences of Pietism and then, most importantly, revivalism.

Christ, you are part of the family, and can enjoy the emotional security our Heavenly Father wants us to experience. Jesus said, "My sheep hear my voice, and I know them, and they follow me: and I give unto them eternal life; and they shall never perish, neither shall any man pluck them out of my hand. My father, which gave them me, is greater than all; and no man is able to pluck them out of my Father's hand" (John 10:27-29).

Note the psychological slant here. A Christian cannot "grow" unless he or she feels secure that he or she can never fall away. At the risk of beating a dead horse here, I want to draw your attention to what this argument presupposes. It presupposes that salvation is a completed "event" that happens at a particular time. It also presupposes that salvation has to do with God's attitude, not man's actual state.

The Orthodox Church rejects the concept of eternal security because She rejects the entire framework that it presupposes. Salvation is a living relationship with God. It cannot be said to have become complete until the resurrection, when Christ will be *all in all*. Remember that God will never override our free will. As long as we are in the flesh, we have the capability to reject God. St. Paul spoke about why he strove so valiantly in the spiritual life:

> *I therefore so run, not as uncertainly; so fight I, not as one that beateth the air: But I keep under my body, and bring it into subjection: lest that by any*

171

means, when I have preached to others, I myself should be a castaway (1 Cor. 9:26-27).

In other words, St. Paul worked at his salvation to attain that for which he hoped. And yet, he knew that he was not working under his own power but in the power of God. Thus he urged the Philippians:

Wherefore, my beloved, as ye have always obeyed, not as in my presence only, but now much more in my absence, work out your own salvation with fear and trembling. For it is God which worketh in you both to will and to do of His good pleasure (Phil. 2:12-13).

The Orthodox do not doubt the power of God. We do not doubt that God is able to keep all that come to Him. *But*, He will not keep them against their will. Salvation must be a *free* relationship, or it is no relationship at all.

At every service the Orthodox pray that they may spend the remainder of their lives in "peace and repentance" and for "a good defense before the dread Judgment Seat of Christ." We pray thus because our ultimate destiny depends not on what God thinks of us — He is love — but upon our spiritual state. Whether we love His appearing or dread it depends upon the state of our soul.

No Orthodox Christian, not even the holiest of spiritual fathers, would presume to say that he has reached the height of perfection in this life. As we said above, the holier one becomes, the more aware one becomes of one's own sinfulness. Therefore, the Christian remains ever vigilant *lest* he fall. But *if* he falls, he knows that God accepts all who return to Him in repentance. How many times is this fall and repentance repeated in a life? Thousands, hundreds of thousands of times.[12]

Once again, I cannot stress strongly enough that God's attitude toward us does not change because we sin. Rather, it is our sin itself that forms a barrier between God and us. As often as a barrier is erected, it must be torn down through repentance. To assume, however, that man cannot be lost blunts the need for repentance.

---

[12] The monastic prayer rule consists of hundreds, if not thousands, of full prostrations during the night. This is taken as a physical image of the need to "get up" and repent after each fall.

Reflection

1. Who do many Evangelicals believe the one can be "assured" of one's salvation?

2. Does 1 John 5:13 mean that each, individual believer can know that he is saved?

3. What does the Protestant doctrine of assurance presuppose?

4. How is this different from the Orthodox approach?

5. Why is humility important?

6. Does the Protestant doctrine of assurance lead to humility or pride?

7. What is the origin of the Protestant doctrine of eternal security?

8. How does it fit within a Calvinist system?

9. How do most Evangelical Protestants view eternal security?

10. Why do the Orthodox reject this idea?

CHAPTER THIRTEEN

The Immortality of the Soul and the Resurrection

Thus in the delightful mansions
*   on the borders of paradise*
do the souls of the just
*   and righteous reside,*
awaiting there
*   the bodies they love,*
so that, at the opening
*   of the Garden's gate,*
both bodies and souls might proclaim,
*   amidst Hosannas,*
"Blessed is He who has brought Adam from
Sheol
*   and returned him to paradise in the com-*
*   pany of many.*[1]

It has become popular in the last forty years or so to draw a sharp distinction between belief in the immortality of the soul and belief in the resurrection of the soul and body at the Second Coming. According to scholars such as Oscar Cullmann, the idea of an immortal soul is the product of Greek philosophy and is fundamentally antithetical to the Christian doctrine of the

---

[1] Ephrem the Syrian, *Hymns on Paradise*, p. 135.

resurrection.[2] Others, in particular Robert Wilken, have
pointed out that belief in some form of immortality has
been present throughout the Christian theology and has
happily coexisted with the doctrine of the resurrection.[3]
What are we to make of this situation? Is there a defini-
tive Orthodox position on the subject?

In general, Church Fathers have taken one of three
possible positions on the issue:

1. The soul is created and therefore mortal. It is
dissolved at death and recreated at the resurrection.

2. The soul is not *naturally* immortal, but is
kept alive by God until the resurrection, when
final immortality will be bestowed upon the
complete man (this might be called "immortality" in a derivative sense).

3. The soul is *naturally* immortal. That is, it possesses immortality as a natural property, although it is created.

The first view may have been held by early Christian apologists such as St. Justin the Philosopher[4],

[2] "Immortality of the Soul or Resurrection of the Dead?" in
Krister Stendahl, ed. *Immortality and Resurrection* (NY: McMillan,
1965), pp. 9-53.
[3] "The Immortality of the Soul and Christian Hope" in *dialog*
15 (Spring, 1976), pp. 110-117.
[4] Cf. *Dialogus cum Tryphone Judeo* 4-6. M. O. Young attributes
this position to Justin based on the *Dialogue with Trypho*: "The doctrine of the death of souls may well have been a theory of his own

Tatian[5], and Theophilus of Antioch.[6] The third view seems to have been held by Origen and St. Augustine[7] and possibly even St. Maximus the Confessor.[8] The majority of Church Fathers, however, fall into the second category. Indeed, as I shall argue below, the second position best reflects the mind of the Church on the matter.

devising, suggested by Stoic beliefs which would have seemed to him the logical alternative to the Platonic immortality he had rejected in becoming a Christian. In any case, he would have been aware that the death of souls was not a doctrine generally taught in the church. Hence his gingerly mention of it. Tatian, being less concerned with orthodoxy, taught it openly and as a fact." "Justin Martyr and the Death of Souls," *Studia Patristica* 16:2 (1985), p. 215.

[5] Cf. Πρὸς Ἕλληνας 6, 13. "The soul is not in itself immortal, O Greeks, but mortal. Yet it is possible for it not to die. If, indeed, it knows not the truth, it dies, and is dissolved with the body, but rises again at last at the end of the world with the body, receiving death by punishment in immortality. But, again, if it acquires the knowledge o f God, it dies not, although for a time it be dissolved."

[6] Cf. *Ad Autolycum* I:8, II:26. The case for Theophilus is probably the weakest of the three, and I remain skeptical that he actually believed in the dissolution of the soul.

[7] Cf. *De Civitate Dei* 13.2:2-7.

[8] Cf. *Four Centuries on Charity* III:25-28. St. Maximus bases the immortality of man solely on the power of God and the fact that God's "gifts are not subject to revision." For Maximus, man's immortality is part of the original image of God; it is an image of God's eternal being, even though, unlike God, man has a beginning.

CHAPTER THIRTEEN

Christianity vs. Hellenism

Before we examine these positions in detail, however, let us consider why the early Christians were not unanimous on the subject of the soul's immortality as they were, for example, on the subject of the resurrection. Some modern Orthodox scholars have presented the belief in the immortality of the soul as an "open and shut case."[9] As we shall see, however, this is a gross oversimplification.

Part of the reason has to do with the fact that there was no consensus within the wider society on the subject. Judaism was in the process of developing its view of the soul, there being no clear-cut position on immortality in the Hebrew Scriptures.[10] Even among the Hellenistic philosophers, there was no consensus. The Platonists taught the doctrine without reservation (in-

[9] Cf. Constantine Carvarnos *Immortality of the Soul* (Belmont, MA: The Institute for Byzantine and Modern Greek Studies, 1993). See also, Fr. Michael Pomazansky, *Orthodox Dogmatic Theology: A Concise Exposition*, tr. by Seraphim Rose (Platina, CA: St. Herman of Alaska Brotherhood, 1994), pp. 130-134.

[10] Cf. Neil Gillman, *The Death of Death: Resurrection and Immortality in Jewish Thought* (Jewish Lights Pub., 1997). St. John Chrysostom states explicitly that the ancient Jews had no clear concept of life after death. For them, immortality was to be found in producing offspring. *On Marriage and Family Life*, tr. by Catharine P. Roth and David Anderson (Crestwood, NY: SVS Press, 1986), p. 85. Fr. Michael Pomazansky's statement, "the idea of immortality is present without and doubt in the Old Testament... (p. 131)" is an overstatement. The survival of the soul is *hinted* at, and the resurrection is *suggested* in a couple of places, but it is not until the time of the Maccabees that we have a clear-cut presentation of belief in the survival of the soul and of resurrection.

cluding the transmigration of souls), but other schools of philosophy taught the death of the soul.[11]

To further complicate matters, those who did teach the immortality of the soul did so from a philosophical position that was unacceptable to the early Christians. For the Hellenists, to say that the soul is immortal was equivalent to saying that the soul is divine. Plato based part of his argument for the immortality of the soul on his concept of knowledge as recollection. How do we know things such as mathematics? We "remember" them from the knowledge we had before we were born into the body. If, therefore, our soul existed before its incarnation, it must also persevere after death.

Behind the Greek notions of the immortality of the soul lies a monistic philosophy that makes no real dis-

---

[11] Homer apparently did not put forth a concept of the "soul" that we would recognize as such. Werner Jaeger, "The Greek Ideas of Immortality," in Stendhal, ed. *Immortality and Resurrection*, pp. 97-114. [This article may also be found in the *Harvard Theological Review* 52:3 (July, 1952), pp. 135-148.] Jaeger states that the concept of the immortality of the soul did not gain currency until the time of the Orphic religion. Orphic religion, along with the Pythagorean concept of the ascetic life, focused on the inner life of man, and, according to Jaeger, set the stage for speculation on the immortality of the soul. Jaeger also asserts that the Orphic religion greatly influenced Empedocles and Plato in their concepts of the transmigration of souls. Others, however, attribute Empedocles' understanding to the influence of the Pythagorean doctrine of metempsychosis. Cf. Kirk, Raven, Schofield, *The Presocratic Philosophers* (Cambridge: Cambridge University Press, 1983 [2nd Ed.]), p. 321.

tinction between the created and the uncreated.[12] This is especially clear in later Platonism (Neo-Platonism), where souls are considered to be an emanation from the One.[13] Such a notion is in direct conflict with the Judeo-Christian notion of creation *ex nihilo* — from nothing. For Christians, there is an irreducible gulf between the Creator, Who is Uncreated and beyond Being, and the creation, which was brought into existence from nothing. It was impossible, therefore, for the early Christians to simply accept the Platonic view of immortality.[14]

Why, then, did *all* of the early Christians not follow Tatian's lead and reject the immortality of the soul outright? We find a significant clue in the letter of Theophilus of Antioch to Autolycus. In section 27 Theophilus lays out the problem:

[12] Cf. C. J. de Vogel, *Philosophia I, Studies in Greek Philosophy* (Philosophical Texts and Studies 19, I 1970), pp. 397-416. See also J. Zizioulas, *Being as Communion* (Crestwood, NY: SVS Press, 1985), p. 29.

[13] In certain places in the *Enneads*, Plotinus draws an almost ontological distinction between the One and all other things. This distinction, however, is far from the Christian distinction between the Uncreated and the created. For Plotinus, the most basic plurality — even the duality between thought and its object — constitutes the difference between the One and all else. Nevertheles, it is clear that all else constitutes an emanation from the One, therefore securing the ontological continuity between souls and the One.

[14] Origen came closest to a Platonic understanding of immortality precisely because he shared the fundamental ontological monism of the Platonists. See Georges Florovsky, "St. Athanasius' Concept of Creation," in *Aspects of Church History*, Vol. 4 in the *Collected Works* (Belmont, MA: Nordland, 1975), pp. 42-47.

But someone will say to us, "Was man created mortal by nature?" Not at all. "Was he then created immortal?" We do not say this either. But someone will say, "Was he then crated as nothing at all?" We do not say this. In fact, man was neither mortal nor immortal by nature. For if God had made him immortal from the beginning, he would have made him God. Again, if he had made him mortal, it would seem that God was responsible for his death. God therefore made him neither immortal nor mortal, but as we have said before, capable of both. If he were to turn to the life of immortality by keeping the commandment of God, he would win immortality as a reward from him and would become a god; but if he turned to deeds of death, disobeying God, he would be responsible for his own death.[15]

Theophilus is caught between a rock and a hard place. He cannot affirm the natural immortality of the soul, for that would be the same as making man a god, but on the other hand he cannot affirm that man is naturally mortal because that would imply that God is responsible for death. There are two problems: the one is philosophical, the other moral.

Of course, Theophilus' solution is not very satisfying philosophically. If one is not immortal, one must

[15] From R. M. Grant's translation, *Theophilus of Antioch: Ad Autolycum* in the *Oxford Early Christian Text* series (Oxford: Oxford University Press, 1970), pp. 69-71,

necessarily be mortal; his attempt at a *via media* seems to violate the principle of non-contradiction. Nevertheless, he was neither the first nor the only theologian to try to straddle fence, as it were.[16]

In addition to the moral problem of appearing to make God the cause of death, the early theologians also had to deal with the question of what happened to the soul between death and the resurrection. This leads us to the second reason why the vast majority of Christian theologians rejected the first approach: both the writers of the New Testament and the liturgy of the Church implied that that there is some sort of conscious survival of the personality after death.

There are numerous passages from the New Testament that speak of the existence of the soul after death. In the parable of Lazarus and the rich man, the dead are not only conscious, but mindful of those left behind on earth (Luke 16:20ff.). While hanging on the Cross, Christ promised the Good Thief that He would be with him in Paradise *that very day* (Luke 23:43) St. Paul states that it is far better to depart this life and be with Christ (Phil. 1:23). The author of Hebrews writes that we are surrounded by a cloud of witnesses (Heb. 12:1). Perhaps most convincingly, St. Peter writes that Christ preached to "the spirits in prison" and that the Gospel was preached to the dead (1 Peter 3:19; 4:16).

In addition, the Church from the earliest times prayed for the dead. There is no doubt that the *primary*

---

[16] According to Jaeger, the idea can be traced back to the Jewish theologian Philo of Alexandria. St. Ephrem the Syrian held an idea similar to that of Theophilus.

impetus for such prayer was the belief in the resurrection and final judgement. It is significant that the first use of the word "resurrection" in the Scriptures occurs in conjunction with prayer for the dead. 2 Maccabees records that after a battle Judas Maccabeus discovered that his slain men had been wearing tokens of idols. He prayed for the souls of his men and made a sin offering in their behalf. It is stated that he did this on account of the resurrection and judgment to come (2 Maccabees 12:43-45). This is the same reasoning behind St. Paul's prayer for Onesiphorus: *the Lord grant unto him that he may find mercy of the Lord in that day* (2 Tim. 1:18).

The theology express in these passages is clearly focused on the resurrection and is not necessarily incompatible with the idea of the dissolution of the soul at death. However, in addition to praying for the deceased that they might find blessedness on the Last Day, the Church also explicitly prays for the dead *in their present state*, especially as the dead undergo what has been called the particular judgment. *The Canon for the Departing of the Soul from the Body*, the funeral hymnography, and the whole notion of serving forty-day liturgies for the dead all imply the continued, conscious existence of the soul after death.[17]

[17] At this point I should say something about the "Toll Houses" that one encounters in the *Cannon for the Departing of the Soul* and in contemporary Orthodox literature on the soul. Fr. Seraphim Rose emphasized the "Toll Houses" in his *The Soul After Death* (St. Herman of Alaska Brotherhood, 1980). This occasioned a sharp critique from Frs. (now Bishop) Lazar Puhalo and Michael Azkoul, who asserted that idea is of Gnostic origin. Two points need to be emphasized in connection with this issue. First of all, *pace* Frs. Puhalo

CHAPTER THIRTEEN

In short, therefore, the tradition of the Church taken as a whole weighs against the idea that that the soul dissolves at death and is recreated at the resurrection.[18] Those writers, such as Tatian, who held this idea are clearly out of the mainstream of Church teaching. Anyone who advances this notion today does so against not only the teachings of the Fathers, but against the liturgical tradition of the Church as well.

and Azkoul, the Toll House imagery *is* a part of the historical tradition of the Church. Second—and Fr. Seraphim Rose says as much—the Toll Houses are *not* real. They are vivid, literary images used to express the spiritual reality of the particular judgment that takes place at death. The Toll House imagery expresses the fact that upon death, the devil, who is the enemy of man and who is portrayed in the Old Testament as the "prosecutor" of heaven, will accuse us of the sins we have committed in this life. This is the devil's last chance to win our souls. That is why we pray, in particular to the Theotokos, who is the first among Christians to be fully deified and glorified in heaven with her Son, that we will be protected from the assaults of the devil at our death. The Toll Houses are simply one, very vivid way of expressing this truth. Although there is much in Fr. Seraphim's book to commend it, I do think that he spends too much time on the Toll Houses and on the stories of visions, etc. A far more balanced book is that by Metropolitan Hierotheos Vlachos, *Life after Death* (Birth of the Theotokos Monastery, 1995). I would also recommend Archbishop Lazar Puhalo's *The Soul, the Body and Death* (Dewdney, Canada: Synaxis Press, 1980). Although I do think Archbishop Lazar overreacts to the issue of the Toll Houses, I am in agreement with his overall presentation.

[18] The same would apply to the notion of "soul-sleep."

THE IMMORTALITY OF THE SOUL

The Nature of the Soul

Does this mean, then that the soul is *immortal?* No. We saw above that the reason why the early Fathers rejected the idea of immortality was theological. *God alone has immortality* (1 Tim. 6:16); to say that the soul is immortal is equivalent to saying that it is divine. The Orthodox doctrine of creation *ex nihilo* and the Church's absolute insistence on the irreducible gulf between the Uncreated and the created precludes any such notion.

Origen certainly held that the soul was naturally immortal. Then again, he also blurred the distinction between Creator and creature and seems to have taught the pre-existence of souls. His attempt at a synthesis between Christian faith and Greek philosophy was a failure, earning him an eventual anathema from the Fifth Ecumenical Council in 553.

St. Augustine also held that the soul was immortal by nature, but, as with so many other aspects of his theology, it is not easy to tell exactly what he meant by that. In his earlier works, such as the *Solioquia* and *De immortalitate animae*, he puts forth clearly Platonic arguments for the immortality of the soul. By the time he writes the *City of God*, however, he is more firmly rooted in the Christian tradition. While he asserts that the soul is naturally immortal[19], he also tries to draw a distinction between the immortality of soul and the immortality of God. For Augustine, immortality does not equal eternality.

---

[19] *De Civitate Dei* 13.2:2-7.

Orthodox theologians can—and have!—criticized Augustine for a number of things, but he cannot be criticized for downplaying the centrality of the doctrine of creation *ex nihilo*. He insists that man is created from nothing. Thus he ends up saying, "immortality is created."[20] Given the philosophy of the time, such a notion would have been non-sensical.

Now, Augustine can either be accused of maintaining a contradiction ("created immortality") or hailed as a philosophical genius for restructuring philosophical categories in much the same way that the Cappadocian Fathers did in the Trinitarian controversies. I suspect, however, that Augustine was not trying to do either. As well versed as he was in Neoplatonism, I seriously doubt if Augustine even realized the paradoxical nature of his statements about the soul. I would characterize Augustine's statements on the immortality of the soul as a "Platonic hangover" from his earlier years.

The case of St. Augustine illustrates the difficulties inherent in trying to recast philosophical doctrines in Christian categories. To be sure, one often encounters the phrase, "immortality of the soul" in Orthodox literature and hymnography.[21] In such cases it is impera-

---

[20] *De Civitate Dei* 13:24:184.

[21] The most obvious example is the *troparion* to St. Mary of Egypt: "By thine actions thou hast taught us to despise the flesh, for it passes away, but to care for the soul, which is immortal..." This hymn could easily be taken in a Platonic or even Manichean sense, if it is not placed within the wider context of Church teaching.

tive to interpret such occurrences within the wider context of the Church's teaching. That is, they must be understood in light of the catholic mind of the Church. Taken in this light, such phrases should not be interpreted as implying the *natural* immortality of the soul, but rather the continued existence of the soul after death (by grace), until the general resurrection, when the whole man, soul and body, will enter eternity.

Reflection

1. What are the three possible Christian approaches to the immortality of the soul.

2. How was the soul viewed by the pagan philosophers?

3. How did this affect the Christian attitude?

4. Why did theologians like Theophilus refrain from denying the immortality of the soul completely?

5. Did many Fathers teach the dissolution of the soul?

6. Did many Fathers teach that the soul is naturally immortal?

7. What does the New Testament say about the condition of the soul after death?

8. How is this reflected in the Church's prayer life?

9. How should Orthodox Christians think about the immortality of the soul?

10. How is the immortality of the soul related to the resurrection?

RECOMMENDED READING

General Studies

Carlton, Clark. *The Faith: Understanding Orthodox Christianity*. Salisbury, MA: Regina Orthodox Press, 1997.

George, Archimandrite. *The Deification as the Purpose of Man's Life*. Mt. Athos, Greece: Holy Monastery of St. Gregorios, 1997.

Lossky, Vladimir. *The Mystical Theology of the Orthodox Church*. Crestwood, NY: St. Vladimir's Seminary Press, 1976.

Pelikan, Jaroslav. *The Christian Tradition: A history of the Development of Doctrine*. 5 Vols. Chicago: University of Chicago Press, 1971-1989).

Rose, Seraphim. *God's Revelation to the Human Heart*. Platina, CA: St. Herman of Alaska Brotherhood, 1987.

Ware, Kallistos. *The Orthodox Way*. Crestwood, NY: St. Vladimir's Seminary Press, 1995.

Vlachos, Hierotheos. *The Illness and Cure of the Soul in the Orthodox Tradition*. Tr. by Effie Mavromichali. Levadia, Greece: Birth of the Theotokos Monastery, 1993.

_____. *Life After Death.* Tr. by Esther Williams. Levadia, Greece: Birth of the Theotokos Monastery, 1995.

_____. *Orthodox Psychotherapy: The Science of the Fathers.* Tr. by Esther Williams. Levadia, Greece: Birth of the Theotokos Monastery, 1994.

Spiritual Biographies

Cavarnos, Constantine. *Anchored in God.* Belmont, MA: Institute for Byzantine and Modern Greek Studies, 1975.

Chondropoulos, Sotos. *Saint Nektarios: A Saint for our Times.* Tr. by Peter and Aliki Los. Brookline: Holy Cross Orthodox Press, 1989.

Hackel, Sergei. *Pearl of Great Price: The Life of Mother maria Skobtsova 1891-1945.* Crestwood, NY: St. Vladimir' Seminary Press, 1981.

Joseph, Elder (of Vatopedi). *Elder Joseph the Hesychast: Struggles, Experiences, Teachings.* Tr. by Elizabeth Theokritoff. Mt. Athos, Greece: The Great and Holy Monastery of Vatopedi, 1999.

Maretta, Thomas, Tr. *The Great Collection of the Lives of the Saints.* 12 Volumes in progress. House Springs, MO: Chrysostom Press, 1994-.

Perekrestov, Peter, Ed. *Man of God: Saint John of Shanghai and San Francisco.* Redding, CA: Nikodemus Orthodox Publication Society, 1994.

The Faith Series
By Clark Carlton

"An indispensable guide!" Archbishop DMITRI of Dallas (OCA).

"The best-written Orthodox catechism ever." Metropolitan ISAIAH of Denver (GOA).

"A Joyous event in the life of the Church." Bishop BASIL of Wichita (AOCA).

The *Faith Series* is the most widely acclaimed Orthodox catechetical series in the English language. Each volume focuses on a different aspect of the Orthodox Christian Faith.

The Faith: Understanding Orthodox Christianity (1995).

The Way: What Every Protestant Should Know About the Orthodox Church (1997).

The Truth: What Every Roman Catholic Should Know About the Orthodox Church (1999).

The Life: The Orthodox Doctrine of Salvation (2000).

Each volume is $22.95 (+ shipping) and is available directly from Regina Orthodox Press: (800) 636-2470.